I0211572

A VERY JEWISH CHRISTMAS CAROL

BY **Elise Esther Hearst** WITH **Phillip Kavanagh**
AFTER **Charles Dickens**

CURRENCY PRESS
The performing arts publisher

MELBOURNE THEATRE COMPANY

CURRENT THEATRE SERIES

First published in 2023
by Currency Press
Gadigal Land, PO Box 2287 Strawberry Hills, NSW, 2012, Australia
enquiries@currency.com.au
www.currency.com.au

in association with Melbourne Theatre Company

Copyright: *A Very Jewish Christmas Carol* © Elise Esther Hearst and Phillip Kavanagh, 2023.

COPYING FOR EDUCATIONAL PURPOSES

The Australian *Copyright Act 1968* [Act] allows a maximum of one chapter or 10% of this book, whichever is the greater, to be copied by any educational institution for its educational purposes provided that that educational institution [or the body that administers it] has given a remuneration notice to Copyright Agency [CA] under the Act.

For details of the CA licence for educational institutions contact CA,
12 / 66 Goulburn Street, Sydney, NSW, 2000; tel: within Australia 1800 066 844 toll free; outside Australia 61 2 9394 7600; fax: 61 2 9394 7601;
email: memberservices@copyright.com.au

COPYING FOR OTHER PURPOSES

Except as permitted under the Act, for example a fair dealing for the purposes of study, research, criticism or review, no part of this book may be reproduced, stored in a retrieval system, or transmitted in any form or by any means without prior written permission. All enquiries should be made to the publisher at the address above.

Any performance or public reading of *A Very Jewish Christmas Carol* is forbidden unless a licence has been received from the author or the author's agent. The purchase of this book in no way gives the purchaser the right to perform the play in public, whether by means of a staged production or a reading. All applications for public performance should be addressed to the author c /-Currency Press at the address above.

Typeset by Brighton Gray for Currency Press.
Cover features Evelyn Krape, Melbourne Theatre Company 2023; photo by Jo Duck.

Currency Press acknowledges the Traditional Owners of the Country on which we live and work. We pay our respects to all Aboriginal and Torres Strait Islander Elders, past and present.

A catalogue record for this book is available from the National Library of Australia

Contents

NEXTSTAGE

Commissioned and developed through Melbourne Theatre Company's NEXT STAGE Writers' Program, supported by our Current and Inaugural Playwrights Giving Circles.

NEXT STAGE positions new Australian works as contenders on the national stage, through strategic investment in stories that reflect our community, are relevant to our times, challenge the boundaries of theatre making and fuel the cultural conversation.

Thank you for sharing our passion and commitment to Australian stories and Australian writers.

CURRENT PLAYWRIGHTS GIVING CIRCLE

Paul and Wendy Bonnici & Family, Tony and Janine Burgess, Kathleen Canfell, Fitzpatrick Sykes Family Foundation, Jane Hansen AO and Paul Little AO, Larry Kamener and Petra Kamener, The Margaret Lawrence Bequest, Helen Nicolay, Tania Seary and Chris Lynch, Craig Semple, Dr Richard Simmie

The Vizard FOUNDATION

INAUGURAL PLAYWRIGHTS GIVING CIRCLE

Louise Myer and Martyn Myer AO, Maureen Wheeler AO and Tony Wheeler AO, Christine Brown Bequest, Allan Myers AC KC and Maria Myers AC, Tony Burgess and Janine Burgess, Dr Andrew McAliece and Dr Richard Simmie, Larry Kamener and Petra Kamener

The Ian Potter Foundation   NAOMI MILGROM FOUNDATION   THE MYER FOUNDATION   MALCOLM ROBERTSON FOUNDATION   THE UNIVERSITY OF MELBOURNE

ELISE ESTHER HEARST is an award-winning Melbourne-based playwright and published author, working and living on Boon Wurrung Country. She studied Creative Arts at Melbourne University and Playwriting at the Royal Court Theatre in London, and was a resident writer with Melbourne Theatre Company in 2019-2020. Her work has appeared at various theatres around Australia, including *Yentl* (Arts Centre Melbourne and Malthouse Theatre in 2024); *The Mesh* (Red Stitch Actors' Theatre); *The Sea Project* (Gri in Theatre); and *Bright World* (Theatre Works). Her debut novel, *One Day We're All Going to Die*, was published in 2023 by HQ Fiction, Harper Collins Australia.

PHILLIP KAVANAGH is a playwright, originally from Adelaide. From 2019-2020, Phillip was a Melbourne Theatre Company resident writer as part of the NEXT STAGE Writers' Program. He completed a Bachelor of Creative Arts (Honours) and a Master of Arts in Creative Writing at Flinders University, as well as a Graduate Diploma of Dramatic Art (Playwriting) at NIDA. He is currently a PhD candidate at Flinders University. His plays include *Jesikah* (State Theatre Company South Australia), *Deluge* (Tiny Bricks/Brink/Adelaide Festival), *Replay* (Griffin Theatre Company) and a new adaptation of Moliére's *Tartuffe* (Brink/State Theatre Company South Australia). Phillip is one-half of the independent theatre company Tiny Bricks, a creative partnership with director Nescha Jelk. He has been awarded the Patrick White Playwrights' Award, Jill Blewett Playwright's Award, and the Colin Thiele Creative Writing Scholarship.

Playwright's Notes

I'd like to preface this note with the following: Charles Dickens is a beloved author to many. *David Copperfield* was among my Holocaust-survivor grandmother's favourite texts. Dickens, a masterful storyteller, also drew unsympathetic, at times anti-Semitic depictions of Jews in his work. While his views were in line with the dominant mentality at the time of his writing, it is impossible for me, as a Jew, not to view his novella *A Christmas Carol*, an indisputable gem of craft and story, through this lens: here we have a belligerent, cruel, miserly man with a love of money named Ebenezer Scrooge, often depicted in illustrations with a hooked nose, who can only be redeemed by embracing his love for Christmas. Read into all of that what you will.

This was not my motivation for writing the play, and before embarking on this project, I can't say I ever gave it that much thought. Like most Aussie children I grew up loving Christmas stories and the plethora of adaptations of *A Christmas Carol* in film and television (also likely owed to the dearth of representations of Chanukah stories in popular culture).

The origin story of this work begins here: Christmas 2019. Co-writer Phillip Kavanagh and I were both resident writers of Melbourne Theatre Company's NEXT STAGE Writers' Program, and I found myself tasked for the first time with making Christmas lunch for my husband's family. In the writers' room, Phil and I were bouncing around ideas of what I would serve and how I would decorate in the same way we might have bandied around ideas for a play. One thing led to another, and in an almost Dickensian way, one morning Phil awoke from a dream and said, 'A Christmas Carol, but make it Jewish'. And so the work began.

But what did it mean to 'make it Jewish'? Well, not to be too obvious about it, but setting it in a bakery felt apt. Jews, after all, adore food, express love through weekly rituals of coming together for Shabbat dinners, and most religious festivals are teeming with symbolic foods; salt water for the tears we shed, round challah for continuity of life, gefilte fish for … well, gefilte fish is not my thing. Anyway, so goes the joke, 'they tried to kill us, we survived, let's eat!'.

In this bakery we find Elysheva Scroogavitz, nine months pregnant and battling her own inexplicable grief – the loss of her fiancé and father of her unborn child. As her story evolves so too do the key familial figures in her life, and this play becomes a multi-generational one, a tussle between Elysheva's free will, and the burden of epigenetic trauma that she carries. When the ghost of Elysheva's Holocaust-survivor grandmother appears, it sets off a supernatural journey and forces her to face not only her own grief, but all the unspoken losses and memories that came before her.

This is a story about ghosts. We all have them, whether they are seen or unseen, talked about or forgotten. For descendants of Holocaust survivors, our ghosts, dybbuks[1] and demons are innumerable. I spent my whole life pestering my grandmother for details of her ghosts, but for her, like so many of her generation who also ended up here in Melbourne, it was too much to speak of.

A Very Jewish Christmas Carol is a comedy. You will laugh, you will plotz[2], and you may cry, but the brief was to make this Christmas show Jewish, and what good Jewish comedy would it be if there wasn't a little tsuris[3]?

So it is a gift that I can present this magical story to you. From the kernel of an idea between two playwrights to a mystical world brought to life by the wizardry and wondrous minds of my fellow theatre makers and dreamers, in particular Sarah Giles, director extraordinaire, and Jennifer Medway, dramaturg extraordinaire, who both held and guided this piece, these survivors, their memories, with love, respect, and technical brilliance. Thank you both for your compassion, wisdom and hilarity. It would not be possible to make this show without its community; please read on in this program for the names of all the brilliant people who made it so. I thank them all from the bottom of my heart. Thank you to Phillip Kavanagh for imagining this world with me. And I thank Melbourne Theatre Company for giving life to these Jewish voices, not merely as side characters or punchlines, but showing them as they are – thunderous beating hearts of Melbourne's eclectic wider community.

Elise Esther Hearst
Lead Writer

---

1   In Jewish folklore, a human spirit that enters and controls a living person.
2   To crack, burst, shatter or explode. Commonly used to refer to a person bursting with emotion.
3   Troubles, problems.

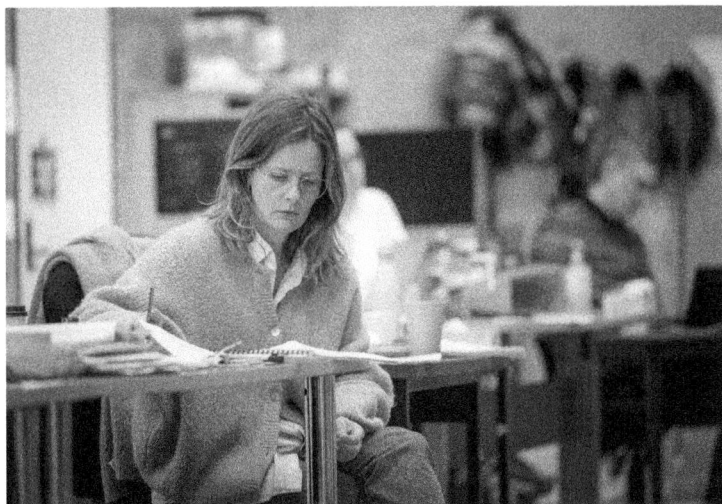

Director Sarah Giles in rehearsal.

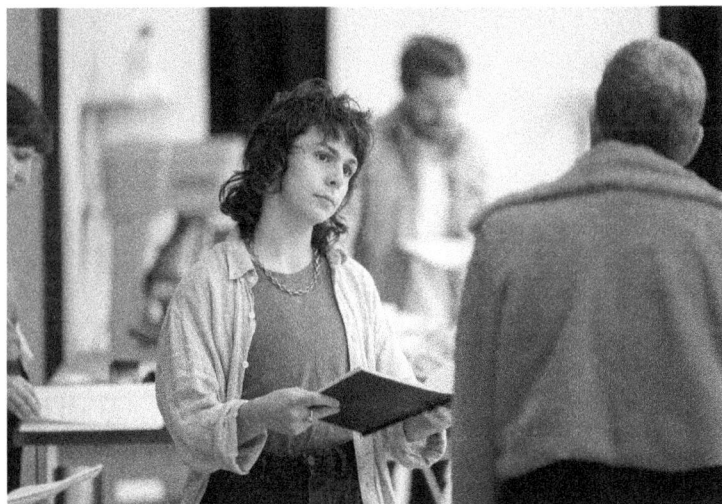

Emma Jevons with Natalie Gamsu in rehearsal.

Evelyn Krape in rehearsal.

Jude Perl (centre), with Emma Jevons and Michael Whalley in rehearsal.

Jude Perl, Louise Siversen, Emma Jevons, Natalie Gamsu, Michael Whalley and Miriam Glaser in rehearsal.

Jude Perl, Louise Siversen, Michael Whalley, Emma Jevons, Evelyn Krape and Natalie Gamsu in rehearsal.

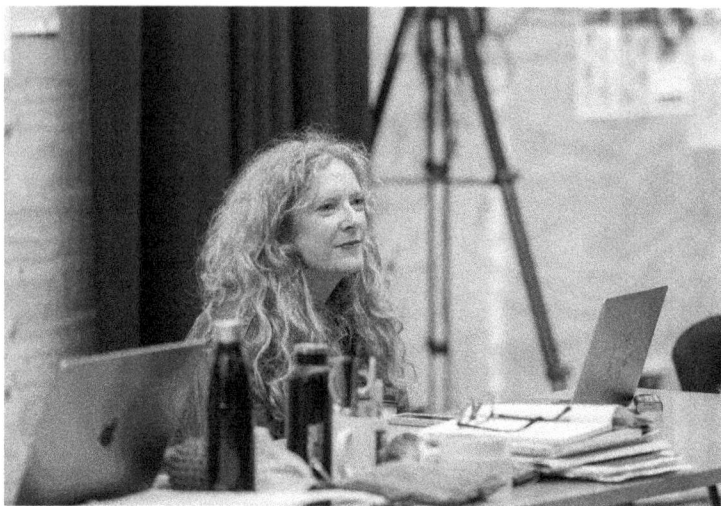

Lead Writer Elise Esther Hearst in rehearsal.

Louise Siversen (centre), with Miriam Glaser and Michael Whalley in rehearsal.

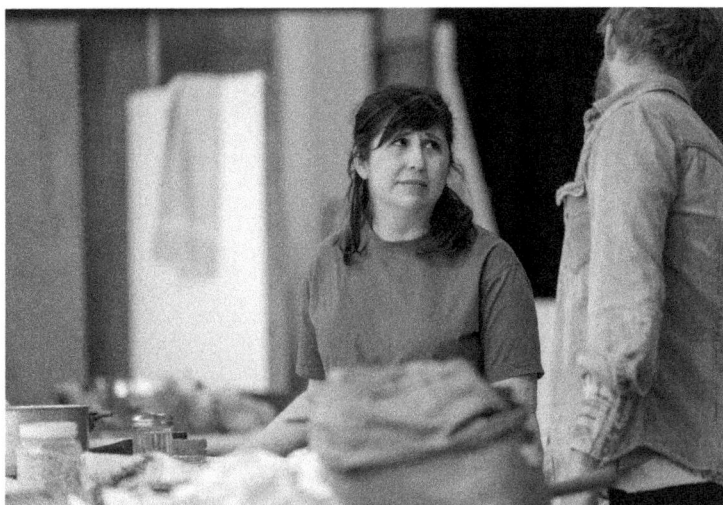

Miriam Glaser with Michael Whalley in rehearsal.

A Very Jewish Christmas Carol was first produced by Melbourne Theatre Company at Southbank Theatre, The Sumner, Melbourne on the lands of the Boon Wurrung and Wurundjeri peoples of the Kulin Nation, on 14 November 2023 with the following cast and creatives:

FRAN / LILITH / ENSEMBLE	Natalie Gamsu
ELY	Miriam Glaser
SARAH / ENSEMBLE	Emma Jevons
BUBI / GOLEM / ENSEMBLE	Evelyn Krape
RIVKA / ENSEMBLE	Jude Perl
CAROL / REIN-DYBBUK / ENSEMBLE	Louise Siversen
BEN / ENSEMBLE	Michael Whalley

Director, Sarah Giles
Associate Director, Cassandra Fumi
Musical Director / Arranger, Jude Perl
Set Designer, Jacob Battista
Costume Designer, Dann Barber
Lighting Designer, Richard Vabre
Design Concept Contributor, Jonathon Oxlade
Additional Composition, Jude Perl
Voice and Text Coach, Matt Furlani
Fight Choreographer, Lyndall Grant
Intimacy Coordinator, Cessalee Stovall
Polish Translation and Language Coach, Krystyna Duszniak
Yiddish Translation, Rebecca (Rivke) Margolis
Yiddish Language Coach, Freydi Mrocki

CHARACTERS

ELY

BUBI, Ely's grandmother

FRAN, Ely's mother

SARAH, Ely's younger sister

RIVKA, a rabbi

BEN, Ely's fiancé

CAROL, Ben's mother

REIN-DYBBUK, a spirit, played by the actor playing Carol

GINGERBREAD GOLEM, a spirit, played by the actor playing Bubi

LILITH CLAUS, a spirit, played by the actor playing Fran

MISHA, Bubi as a young woman, played by the actor playing Sarah

ADA, Bubi's friend in Poland, played by the actor playing Rivka

RENIA, Bubi's mother, played by the actor playing Fran

HALINA, Bubi's grandmother, played by the actor playing Carol

JAKOB, Bubi's brother, played by the actor playing Ben

THE CAROLLERS, played by everyone interchangeably

NOTE

The ghosts of ADA and BEN may appear throughout the show.

This play text went to press before the end of rehearsals and may differ from the play as performed.

SCENE ONE

Ada's Bakery. Christmas and Chanukah Eve.

A large commercial kitchen, very messy, trays and trays of gingerbread people. A large clock is on the wall. It is 5:59 p.m. Appliances include industrial-sized oven and fridge. There is a counter window where customers are served, and the display cases are pretty much empty, maybe a few flies buzzing around, a sign that reads: 'Everything Half Price'. There is a door to the street. The door dings when it opens. There is a broom closet, from where we can see clothes spilling out of a suitcase, takeaway containers. It is unkempt, messy, squalor.

ELY *is nine months pregnant. She is working on a life-sized gingerbread person.*

ELY *tries the latest batch of dough. It tastes terrible.*

ELY: Oy humbug.

> *Beat.*

You did this.

> *The door swings open, and the Chrismakkah* CAROLLERS *are standing there. They start to perform a Chrismakkah song.*

We're closed.

> ELY *slams the door shut.*

> *The door swings open and* FRAN *enters.*

FRAN: [*to* CAROLLERS] Don't mind her. Keep going!

> *The* CAROLLERS *continue singing.*

ELY: I said we're closed.
FRAN: But the sign says—
ELY: Forget about the sign. Closed.
FRAN: Well hallelujah.
ELY: What does that mean?
FRAN: It means I'm glad you're closed.
ELY: I'm not closed.
FRAN: But you said—

ELY: I'm closed to tone-deaf / losers like—

FRAN: Sh! Sh! Sh! Ely, please don't make a scene in front of the Chrismakkah Carollers. I brought them here especially for you.

ELY: Well can you make them leave especially for me?

FRAN: [*to* CAROLLERS] She's joking, she loves music. [*To* ELY] You love music! The Chrismakkah carols were your favourite. What was that one you came up with? 'Judolf the Red-Nosed Maccabee'?

ELY: Not likely.

FRAN: Such a clever arrangement, people just loved it.

ELY: I hate people.

> ELY *picks up a tray of gingerbread and hurls it at the* CAROLLERS. *A* CAROLLER *picks a gingerbread up off the ground to try.*

FRAN: [*to* CAROLLER] Oh! I wouldn't eat that if—

> *The* CAROLLER *spits out the gingerbread and discreetly puts it in their pocket.*

ELY: Out.

> FRAN *turns to the* CAROLLERS.

FRAN: I'm so sorry about this.

ELY: Leave.

FRAN: Maybe next year.

ELY: Go.

CAROLLERS: Sorry, Ely. Sorry. Bye, Fran. Bye.

ELY: And don't come back!

> *The* CAROLLERS *leave.*

FRAN: That actually went better than I expected.

ELY: No it didn't. You're still here.

FRAN: I'm choosing not to take that personally.

ELY: You should take that personally.

FRAN: So can I turn the sign over to closed then?

ELY: Don't touch that sign.

FRAN: 'Don't touch that sign.' God forbid I touch the sign. Hashem will punish us all! For goodness' sakes, Elysheva. It's Chrismakkah Eve!

ELY: What?

FRAN: It's Chrismakkah Eve.

ELY: Chrismakkah isn't happening.

FRAN: No?

ELY: No.

FRAN: Right. And the other thing?

ELY: What other thing?

FRAN: It's also …

ELY: What.

FRAN: Well I thought today was …

ELY: What?!

FRAN: Your due date.

ELY: What did you call me?

FRAN: Oh, Elysheva. My love. My first daughter. You're my everything, you know.

ELY: What about Sarah?

FRAN: She's my other everything.

ELY: Uh-huh.

FRAN: You shouldn't be alone.

ELY: I'm not alone. I'm at one with the ghosts of the bakery.

FRAN: Do not joke about such things, Elysheva! The spirit world is nothing to be laughed at.

ELY: Don't start.

FRAN: [*seeing the large gingerbread person*] And what is this … this … what is this you are working on?

ELY: Oh. I'm trying something new.

FRAN: Oh good. So you're not still trying to figure out the recipe then?

ELY: Of course I'm trying to figure out the recipe. What else would I be doing?

FRAN: Well it's just a rather unusual way of going / about it.

ELY: Okay bye!

FRAN: Bye? You can't get rid of me that easily.

ELY: I'll say this as nicely as possible. Mum. Please piss ohhh—

ELY *holds on to the bench.*

FRAN: What is it?

ELY: Sh!

FRAN: Is it the baby? A contraction? Did it kick? And if it did kick please let me touch it, please! You see Elysheva you need your mother here you need / me to—

ELY: It was nothing. And let me make this very, very clear. This isn't happening. And neither is Chrismakkah.

SARAH *enters the bakery carrying laundry.*

SARAH: Happy Chrismakkah Eve, every—

FRAN *starts emphatically shaking her head.*

No, no it's not it's just another day of the year and—
FRAN: That's right. Just another day God help me, Sarah.
SARAH: Fresh undies!

SARAH *puts the laundry down.*

FRAN: I did her undies yesterday.
SARAH: Geez she goes through a lot of undies.
FRAN: It's the pressure on the bladder and the urethra and the pelvic floor. You were like a giant watermelon pushing right / down on my—
SARAH: [*to* ELY] How are you, sister? [*Answering for* ELY] Oh me? I'm great. Just here in my usual spot. Making mounds and mounds of inedible gingerbread. Or in this case … a giant gingerbread? [*To* FRAN] Um … Mum … Everything okay here?
FRAN: Oh. You know. No more okay than usual.
SARAH: So … less okay then?
FRAN: Yes.
SARAH: You don't think she's trying to make a replica of …
ELY: What?
SARAH / FRAN: Nothing.
SARAH: Is Carol coming?
FRAN: Unfortunately. Sorry, that was rude. I just … hate Carol.
SARAH: Oh we all hate Carol.
FRAN: She's just too excited about Christmas. When other people tell me their plans for Christmas I feel a glow of warmth. When Carol talks about Christmas it feels like a hate crime.

CAROL *enters wearing Christmassy clothes and a reindeer headband.*

CAROL: Yoo hoo! Merry Christmas…kah to one and all! Ely! Franny! Sarah!
FRAN / SARAH: Carol.

FRAN: Speak of the devil.

CAROL: Ha! You lot are just hilarious!

SARAH: Oh, you know us Jews. Always cracking jokes.

CAROL: Yes. Often professionally. How are you, Sarah?

SARAH: Who me? Oh. Thanks for asking / I'm—

CAROL: That's wonderful dear, and where's the mother-to-be be be ...

Sees the giant gingerbread person and gets a fright.

Ahh! Jesus, Mary and Joseph what on earth is that you're making, Ely?! Scared the living daylights out of me!

FRAN: Get a hold of yourself, Carol. It's just a gingerbread.

SARAH: A giant gingerbread. Person. Right, Ely?

ELY: What?

SARAH / FRAN: Nothing.

CAROL: Sorry, Fran. I never know with you lot whether things are what you say they are.

FRAN: How do you mean?

CAROL: Well if things are normal, or Jewish ... normal. No ... that didn't come out right ... Oh, you know what I mean, Franny.

FRAN: No. No, I don't.

CAROL takes a soft reindeer toy out of her bag.

CAROL: Neigh!

SARAH: Why is Carol neighing?

CAROL: It's a reindeer! For the baby! I thought Ely could take it to hospital. Grandmothers, Franny. We're going to be grandmothers!

SARAH: Do reindeers neigh?

FRAN: [*to* SARAH] How should I know? [*To* CAROL] Thank you, Carol. I'll take that for Ely.

FRAN discreetly puts the toy in the bin.

CAROL: And who's excited for Christmas...kah tomorrow? Ely?

FRAN: Turns out it's a bit of a touchy / subject

CAROL: And you know what I thought would be cute, Franny? The Christmas...kah Carollers. And as a favour to little old me they might do a one-night-only— Oh! Maybe I could join in! Carol and the Christmas...kah Carollers! Carol and the Carollers. Or maybe just ... Carol!

FRAN: No Carol. Terrible idea. And for the last time it's Chrismakkah. Chrismakkah.

CAROL: That's what I said. Christmas…kah.

> RIVKA *enters.*

RIVKA: Hello, Scroogavitzes!

FRAN / SARAH: Rabbi Rivka.

RIVKA: [*to* FRAN] Chag sameach.

FRAN: Chag sameach, Rivka.

RIVKA: [*to* SARAH] Gut yontif.

SARAH: Gut yontif.

RIVKA: [*to* ELY] Ely.

ELY: …

RIVKA: Gut yontif. Do we say gut yontif on Chrismakkah? Why not?

SARAH: Not.

RIVKA: Not?

SARAH: We're keeping Chrismakkah on the down low.

RIVKA: I see.

FRAN: So glad you could make it, rabbi.

CAROL: She's the rabbi? I thought rabbis all had big—

SARAH / FRAN: Don't say it.

CAROL: Beards.

RIVKA: You must be Carol. And it is so nice to meet you. I've heard a lot about you.

CAROL: Really? That's funny. I've heard nothing about you. [*To* FRAN] Fran, if I'd known you were bringing your rabbi, I'd have brought my priest.

FRAN: Rivka is merely here to mediate.

CAROL: But my priest could also mediate.

FRAN: But Rivka is here now.

ELY: Mediate what?

FRAN / SARAH / CAROL / RIVKA: Nothing!

CAROL: At the very least you could meet my priest before the baptism.

FRAN: Carol, for the last time, we are not having a baptism.

CAROL: Just a little splash.

FRAN: No.

CAROL: A trickle.

FRAN: No. I've told you. If it's a boy there will be a circumcision at eight days …

CAROL: The horror!

FRAN: Rabbi? A little help …

RIVKA: Me?

FRAN: Who else?

RIVKA: Yeah okay! Well. Circumcision. Brit Milah. The covenant between Abraham and God. An everlasting pact, where all babies born with a …

FRAN: Penis?

RIVKA: … shall have their …

CAROL: Foreskin!

RIVKA: … removed at eight days. It is one of the less … um … pleasant aspects of Judaism. I mean, not for us, am I right, ladies?

Awkward silence.

Does Ely know what she's having?

FRAN: I'm not confident Ely even knows she's having. Ely?

SARAH / CAROL / RIVKA: Ely?

ELY: I'm pregnant?

FRAN: God help me. Rabbi?

RIVKA: Do you have a birth plan, Ely?

ELY: Yep.

SARAH: So what is your plan?

ELY: I'll call an Uber.

SARAH: An Uber?

CAROL: Not to be a pain, Ely dear. But I'd be worried about how it will affect your rating.

FRAN: And then what? The Uber takes you to the hospital I presume?

ELY: Sounds about right.

SARAH: And then what? Come back here and keep working?

ELY: Correct.

SARAH: I was joking.

ELY: I wasn't.

FRAN: What happened to the cot I gave you? And the change table? And the car seat? And the snuggle-wuggle?

ELY: I sold them on Gumtree.

FRAN: You what?!

ELY: They kept threatening to turn off the water. And the gas. And the electricity.

FRAN: What about the protective amulet I gave you?

ELY: Some sucker paid me three hundred bucks for that one.

CAROL: You can find the most interesting things on Gumtree.

FRAN: Toi toi toi! Oh Ely, without the amulet to protect you, Lilith could come in the night and take your child. Or worse, she could take you! Am I right, Rabbi?

RIVKA: Er … I'm not one hundred percent / sure about—

CAROL: What's all this?

FRAN: Lilith. She's a baby-snatching demon / who also …

SARAH: Please don't / say it …

FRAN: Steals semen from teenage boys and impregnates herself.

SARAH: Why? Just why?

RIVKA: Actually, Fran if I / may—

CAROL: Your culture is so fascinating.

FRAN: Listen, Ely, if Lilith arrives, throw some salt in her face.

RIVKA: No, no, no.

ELY: Sure, Mum. If Adam's demonic first wife arrives to claim my unborn child, I'll season her with salt.

CAROL: Adam?

RIVKA: Garden of Eden Adam.

CAROL: Oh! From the Old Testament!

RIVKA: We don't call it / that but …

FRAN: I'm telling you Ely, don't take this stuff for granted.

RIVKA: Sorry if I could just interject …

SARAH: Please do!

RIVKA: Oh. Well. Thank you, Sarah.

SARAH: You're welcome, Rivka.

RIVKA: [*nervously laughing*] Uh yes. Well. Um. So …

CAROL: I hope she's a bit more articulate in church, Franny.

FRAN: Carol, I swear …

RIVKA: Lilith can be powerful. Terrifyingly powerful. Think wild winds. Hurricanes eclipsing the earth …

FRAN: You see? I read on a website / that—

RIVKA: But but but—

FRAN: There's a but?

SARAH: Let the rabbi speak!

RIVKA: There are some schools of thought that suggest Lilith wasn't a demon after all. That she was a force for good, protecting women and their unborn children. I mean, come on, it's the classic trope of strong-lady-who-knows-what-she-wants equals scary demon.

FRAN: But the amulet!

RIVKA: The amulet you speak of may provide some comfort however if it's demons you're worried about, Fran, I'd be looking further afield. Now a dybbuk. That's a bad news demon. A possessor of bodies. Hell-bent on destruction.

CAROL: She's quite an animated rabbi, isn't she?

RIVKA: Or a golem. Well, haha, golems can be forces for good or evil. They're like a kind of man-made or woman-made (am I right) bodyguard, designed to protect Jews from …well … you know.

CAROL: From what?

FRAN: Read a history book, Carol.

CAROL: Which period?

FRAN: Anywhere in the last two thousand years should be a good start.

RIVKA: Then there's Azazel. Oh they're a goodie. Okay so you've got a goat—

CAROL *begins to weep.*

SARAH: Carol's crying. Again.

FRAN: Yes. She does that.

CAROL: WHY? Why oh why?

RIVKA: Why? Why indeed. The most Jewish question a person could ask.

CAROL: Why do bad things happen to good people?

RIVKA: Another zinger, Carol. It reminds me of the sermon I gave the other week on Jews and suffering. I'd be happy to send it around to / anyone who—

FRAN: I'm definitely suffering. There, there, Carol. There, there.

RIVKA: Let it out, Carol.

CAROL: Oh, you're a nice rabbi!

RIVKA: What did you— What did she think / I was—

CAROL: And you, Franny. You're not my flesh and blood. But you're still family. My chosen family. My chosen people.

FRAN: Really?

CAROL: Oh Ely! We just love you! Treasure every moment. Because you never know if ... if ... if ...

RIVKA: Ely, I think what Carol is trying to say is ... We're all just worried about you. And ... we're just trying to help you, right Fran?

FRAN: That's right, Rabbi.

RIVKA: Right Carol?

CAROL: Oh yes, Rabbi.

RIVKA: Right Sarah?

SARAH: ...

FRAN: Sarah?

SARAH: Uh yeah. Sure.

FRAN: Sarah ...

SARAH: Alright! You know we would do anything to help you, Ely.

ELY: You know what? I would actually love your help.

SARAH: What can I do?

ELY: Put on some gloves.

> SARAH *does.*

A hairnet.

> SARAH *does.*

An apron.

> SARAH *does.*

Grab that rolling pin.

> SARAH *does.*

And go fuck yourself.

SARAH: Cool. Real cool.

CAROL: Just put it out of its misery and let the bakery die!

FRAN: Good one, Carol. So we're doing it now I suppose?

SARAH: Thanks a lot, Carol.

CAROL: Well, excuse me!

RIVKA: It's alright, Carol—

ELY: Doing what?

FRAN / SARAH / CAROL: Nothing!

RIVKA: Not nothing. This isn't nothing.

FRAN: No, Rabbi. You're right. This isn't nothing.

CAROL: It's everything.

FRAN: It's time to close the bakery.

ELY: I told you I'm not closing tonight!

FRAN / CAROL: Close it for good!

ELY: What is this? An intervention?

FRAN: We weren't going to call it that.

ELY: Wait what?

CAROL: Sorry, Ely.

ELY: Sarah, you don't agree with this bullshit, do you?

SARAH: I mean …

FRAN: Sarah!

SARAH: She's just really scary when she's angry.

RIVKA: It's important to be honest, Sarah.

ELY: Sarah?

SARAH: Close the bakery, Ely. For good.

ELY: Traitor!

SARAH: But think of it this way. No-one's gonna miss it. There's literally no-one here.

CAROL: Because this place is so barren. There's no Christmas cheer. Where's the tinsel? The mistletoe. Where's the tree?

FRAN: Carol, we've been through this. We don't celebrate Christmas.

CAROL: Not even at Christmas?

FRAN / SARAH: No!

FRAN: Rabbi?

RIVKA: So … okay. Really? Where do I / even …

CAROL: Do not take this from me, Fran. You people have so many holidays, do not take Christmas away from me.

FRAN: You people?

SARAH: Mum! Carol! Time out! Focus!

FRAN: Elysheva. It's time to shut it down. Let it go.

CAROL: Yes, let your bakery go! Oh! I sound just like Moses!

ELY: Of course you'd say that, Mum. You've always hated it.

FRAN: This gingerbread nonsense has been going on for months now. I wish to God my horrible, rude, selfish mother—may her memory be for a blessing—would have written down the recipe, but did she ever do anything I asked her to? No. Of course she didn't. She was so incapable of love and of thinking about anyone else but—

SARAH: Mum. Get to the point.

FRAN: Ely. The bakery is over. It's done. Kaput. Finito. And that's okay. Because we're here. Together we will figure out the next steps. The important thing now is your health and your baby's health. Am I right, Rabbi?

RIVKA: Absolutely. It reminds me of a sermon I delivered / about—

FRAN: And trust me, being here, in this miserable, soul-crushing, life-sucking … oh … oh … did you feel that? It's like my mother is here … the malevolence, the cruelty, the mocking. Mum! Mum! I won't let you do this!

SARAH: Mum! Get a grip!

FRAN: No, Sarah! I won't stand for it. I won't watch her destroy her life. My mother already did that. She dropped dead right where Ely is standing now, smack bang in a pile of dough. I can still see it now, the impression of her stricken face carved into an unbaked loaf of caraway seeded rye. Elysheva, history repeats, and yet does not have to repeat itself. Do you hear me?

CAROL: Amen.

FRAN: I have cleared out the front of the house for you and the baby. We'll get you out of here and you'll move in with me.

CAROL: Or me! I have a whole nursery / set up with—

FRAN: You are not alone. Let me take care of you.

CAROL: Or me, Ely. And if you don't like Scandinavian design we can go with whatever you feel is right.

FRAN: I was all alone when I gave birth to you, Ely, my darling.

SARAH: Okay, Mum. We've all heard the sob story before.

FRAN: I cut my own umbilical cord.

SARAH: Mum.

FRAN: I basically had to do it with my teeth.

RIVKA: Really?

FRAN: And / then I—

SARAH: We just want what's best for you, Ely. Bubi would understand. She didn't leave you the bakery knowing you'd wind up a single mum. And Ben / wouldn't—

ELY: Ben?

CAROL: Ben. My Ben …

FRAN: Ben would have just wanted to see you happy.

RIVKA: I mean, I didn't know Ben personally, / but—

ELY: Oh can you all just be quiet? Do you not hear yourselves?

FRAN: My hearing is / perfectly—

ELY: Enough with your 'caring' and your 'worrying' and your 'being here'. You're right. This bakery is closed.

FRAN: But you said—

ELY: Closed to you. To all of you. Please leave.

FRAN: Ely, you don't mean that. You need us.

ELY: I don't need you. Any of you. Have I not made this clear? Leave! Go! I don't want you here! I just want to be left alone.

FRAN: But we're your family.

ELY: My family? My family? Get this through your heads. There will be no Chrismakkah tomorrow. No Christmas. No Chanukah. There will be me. Here. And I will figure out this gingerbread recipe regardless of how long it takes, even if the baby drops out of me and onto a pile of flour. I don't care what you think: that I can't look after myself, that I destroyed Bubi's bakery, that I don't have a home because I can't go back to the house I used to live in with my dead fiancé. Newsflash. Bubi left this place to me. And why do you think that is? I don't know? Maybe, Mum, it's because you think you're like this sweet ball of dough waiting to be moulded and shaped and loved and devoured, when in reality you are way beyond your use-by date, you know, when the mould has a mind of its own and it spreads and clings on and clings on, desperate for another chance of a life. And Sarah, you're not even dough. No, you're just yeast. Off yeast. You're a yeast infection! For the last time, I am not leaving. You are. There's the door.

FRAN: Oh, Elysheva. That's an awful thing to say to your family.

ELY: Ben was my family. Ben is dead. My family is dead. The end.

Silence.

CAROL: Well … if you don't mind me, I have some last-minute gender-neutral wallpapering to tend to…

CAROL *goes to leave. She turns back.*

Fran … perhaps you'd like to help me choose between the eggshell and the beige?

FRAN: I …

CAROL: Fran? Franny? Come on Franny.

FRAN: Ely? You don't mean it.

>ELY *ignores her.*

FRAN: Yes. Yes. Alright. Coming.

CAROL: [*to* FRAN, *as they are leaving*] You know, I always thought Ely and I had a very good relationship. I hate to say it, but maybe the cliché about difficult daughter-in-laws is true.

FRAN: [*to* CAROL] I think the cliché is about mother-in-laws but …

CAROL: [*to* FRAN] I hope she gets rid of that giant gingerbread. Mildly concerning if you ask me.

FRAN: [*to* CAROL] No-one asked you.

>FRAN *leaves with* CAROL.

>RIVKA *turns to speak to* SARAH *without* ELY *listening.*

RIVKA: On that note …

SARAH: You're leaving?

RIVKA: I didn't think staying was an option. Unless … you need me to stay?

>RIVKA *reaches out her hand to* SARAH. SARAH *shakes her head.*

SARAH: Better not.

RIVKA: Right. Sure. Of course not.

SARAH: That isn't what I meant.

RIVKA: I know what you meant.

SARAH: Thanks for trying.

RIVKA: Just doing my job. I am the rabbi, aren't I?

SARAH: Rivka …

>RIVKA *leaves.*

You happy now? They're all gone.

ELY: You're not.

SARAH: Yeast infection?

ELY: A fucking intervention?

SARAH: I'm pretty sure that's not how interventions are supposed to go …

ELY: You're meant to be keeping all that away from me.

SARAH: I tried my hardest, Ely. You'd better believe I've been trying my hardest for the last nine months. But you won't let me in. You won't talk about the bakery. You won't talk about the pregnancy. You won't talk about Ben.

ELY: That jerk. Of all the things to die of— How can a man make it to his thirties without knowing he's allergic to bees? Who does that?

SARAH: Ben?

ELY: I want to kill him for what he's done to me.

SARAH: Is that— gonna choose not to dwell on the logic of that sentence.

ELY: I hate him!

SARAH: Yes, okay, and you're very angry. Maybe so angry you can't see that things are not good. Mum's a mess, Carol's a mess. I'm … well I'm … well … there's also some stuff that's been happening in my life.

ELY: I don't know how that's possible, you're always bloody here.

SARAH: Only because you need me to be!

ELY: Yeah right.

SARAH: Pass me the flour, Sarah. Clean the oven, Sarah. Empty the bin, Sarah. I'm always here! For you!

ELY: So don't be. Can you lift that tray up for me? I can't seem to bend down …

SARAH *starts to lift the tray for* ELY.

SARAH: Like. I do have a life outside of you, you know.

ELY: Good. Go live it then.

SARAH *deliberately drops the tray to the ground.*

SARAH: For God's sake, Ely. I love you, but you're making it pretty bloody hard to love you.

ELY: Don't bother, then.

SARAH: I don't think you really want this. To be rid of all of us? Come on, Ely. What if your waters break and you're all alone?

ELY: But I am alone. I am alone, Sarah. Ben was my world. And now my world has died. I will never not be alone again.

SARAH: Are you sure about that?

ELY: Why are you still here?

SARAH: Fine. Good luck with all of that then.

SARAH *leaves.*

SCENE TWO

ELY: Luck. I don't need luck. I don't need anyone …

> ELY *tries to pick up the tray. She bends down, can't do it.*

I just need …

> *She manoeuvres herself awkwardly to try and grab it again from a different angle.*

Things to be …

> *She still can't get it.*

Nicer to me!

> *She kicks the tray away from her.*

This is all your fault!

> *The Chrismakkah* CAROLLERS *appear outside and start singing.*

Oh no. Not again. Not today.

> *She heads to the door, opens it.*

Shut up!

CAROLLERS: Sorry, Ely. Sorry.

ELY: You sound like ten … dying … I'm too pregnant to complete this simile.

> *She slams the door shut. Then, the door jingles as if it has been opened. She turns to face the door. Suddenly,* BUBI's *face appears there.*

Bubi!

> BUBI *disappears.* ELY *shakes herself off.*

What? Ha ha ha no. It wasn't her. Okay great. I'm hallucinating. This is all your fault, you anaphylactic disaster. Now look what you've done you've—

> *All the appliances turn on, shake, and make a lot of noise.*

What the—

> *She rushes around, tries to turn things off but the noise intensifies.*

What the hell is happening?!?!

Silence. Everything stops.

That was weird.

The oven starts to shake and whir.

Huh?

The oven door slides open, and BUBI *bursts out of it.* ELY *and* BUBI *stare at each other in disbelief, then both start to scream.*

Get away from me!

BUBI: No you get away from me!

ELY: I'm calling the police!

BUBI: Calling the police on your grandmother? Good luck with that.

ELY: My grandmother. It's not possible she died three years ago so I must be I must be dreaming …

BUBI: Yes, that's right. You're right. I'm dead. I'm dead. I'm dead. I'm dead.

ELY: Stop saying that!

BUBI: Hang on. Are you dead too?

ELY: Am I? Am I dead? When did I die? Hang on, I'm dead. And I'm in hell. Oh, this all make so much sense now.

BUBI: Jews don't believe in hell.

ELY: We don't?

BUBI: I don't know.

ELY *and* BUBI *scream.*

ELY: Stop screaming!

BUBI: You stop screaming!

ELY: What are you?

BUBI: What do you think I am? Chopped liver?

ELY: Bubi?

BUBI: Nu?

ELY: Bubi!

ELY *rushes at* BUBI *and hugs her.*

Bubi, Bubi, Bubi! I can't believe it's you. It's really you!

BUBI: Okay, calm down, Elysheva. I may be dead but that hasn't made me a hugger. And oy vey have you eaten the entire bakery?

ELY: I'm pregnant!

BUBI: Ugh. Children are the worst.

ELY: God I've missed you. And you have no idea what I've been through. They're all so bloody demeaning and patronising and annoying!

BUBI: Who?

ELY: Well, Mum for starters.

BUBI: See? The worst.

ELY: She wants me to close the bakery!

BUBI: My bakery?

ELY: Well, it's technically my bakery, since you left it to / me and all …

BUBI: [*looking around*] Elysheva, what have you done to my bakery?

ELY: What do you mean?

BUBI: Where are all the customers?

ELY: They … are … sleeping?

BUBI: At this time of year there used to be lines of people, not around the block but around the suburb, and then the next suburb! And what the hell is that???

ELY: It's a giant gingerbread?

BUBI: I'm going to kill myself.

ELY: You're already dead!

BUBI: I just got here and she's already giving me a headache.

ELY: Oh. I'm the problem.

BUBI: Yes. You're the problem.

ELY: You're haunting *me*.

BUBI: You think I want to be here? I was having a great time up there. Playing bridge, gorging myself on all-you-can-eat herring, talking loudly at the movies, farting loudly at the movies, especially after the herring …

ELY: I thought you'd be happy to see me.

BUBI: Sure, sure darling. You tell yourself what you need to. But let's just say I was on a Mahjong winning streak and I need to kick Minnie Finklestein's tuchus, oy she thinks she's all that …

ELY: Bubi!

BUBI: I knew that boy was no good for you. He knocks you up and this whole place turns to crap! Where is that no-goodnik?

ELY: You don't know?

BUBI: Don't know what?

ELY: He's dead, Bubi.

BUBI: Dead?

ELY: Yes.

BUBI: The smiley one with the idiot face and that god-awful singing? He's dead?

ELY: Yes. That one.

BUBI: Oh, Elysheva.

ELY: I know.

BUBI: I told you he was a loser!

ELY: Hey!

BUBI: And now you're lumped with the loser mother.

ELY: Carol?

BUBI: Don't let her get her hooves stuck into you. Sleep with one eye open!

ELY: She's not that— Okay she is that bad …

BUBI: Oy, this is worse than I thought.

ELY: It's all going to be fine.

BUBI: Fine? It doesn't look all that fine to me. What's that towel by the sink? Elysheva, do not tell me you are sleeping here.

ELY: The sink is surprisingly easy to wash in. I just attach this little hose and—

BUBI: I'm going to kill myself!

ELY: Bubi. Everything will be fine. It will be. Because you're here now.

BUBI: Why am I here?

ELY: To give me the recipe, of course!

BUBI: What?

ELY: The recipe, Bubi! Your gingerbread recipe. Yes, you've been sent here to save the bakery. We'll get the customers back, I know it. Wanna get your hands dirty and give me a little tutorial now? It's not like you've got anything else going on.

BUBI: No. That can't be right.

ELY: Let me find you an apron. Here. Catch!

   ELY *throws an apron to* BUBI *and* BUBI *doesn't catch it.*

BUBI: You're in some deep shit, Elysheva.

ELY: So just give me the gingerbread recipe! You promised it to me!

BUBI: Did I?

ELY: And if you give it to me I'll save the bakery and then I'll figure out the rest.

BUBI: Figure out the rest?

ELY: You figured it out! You came from nothing and you made / everything.

BUBI: You know nothing about / me.

ELY: And you did it all on your / own.

BUBI: Elysheva …

ELY: And so will / I.

BUBI: You don't want to be alone.

ELY: I do. I absolutely do want to be alone.

BUBI: You think you know it all.

ELY: I really don't know it all which is why you need to give me the recipe!

BUBI: You don't want to end up like me.

ELY: What are you talking about? You were happy. A little on the cranky side. Prone to fits of rage, sure. But you were awesome. I worshipped you. I—

BUBI*'s body is suddenly possessed by an ancient ancestor.*

BUBI: [*Yiddish*] Enough, Elysheva! Do not presume to have all the answers. Instead, learn to ask the questions. Tonight, this Chrismakkah Eve, you'll be visited by three spirits, each one presenting you with a vision of your past, your present, and the future yet to come. Expect the first when the oven bell dings one. The second will come when the oven bell dings two, the third when the oven bell dings three.

BUBI *comes back into her own voice and body.*

[*To* ELY] Did you understand any of that?

ELY: Strangely, I did.

BUBI: Good. Enough already. Now sort yourself out so I never have to return to this godforsaken place. Minnie Finklestein I'm coming for you.

ELY: Don't go! Please don't go Bubi.

BUBI: Och, such a needy child. Into bed.

BUBI *tucks* ELY *into bed.*

Look at you.

ELY: What?

BUBI: Your hair. Your clothes.

ELY: It's not that bad.

BUBI: Az di moyd iz mies zogt zi, der shpigl iz shuldik.

ELY: What?

BUBI: If a girl is ugly, she blames it on the mirror. Would it kill you to make an effort? At least for your daughter's sake.

ELY: I'm having a girl?!

BUBI: So they say.

ELY: Just give me the recipe, Bubi. That's all / you have to—

BUBI: You're going to fall asleep now.

> BUBI *magics* ELY *to sleep.*

Finklestein! I'm on my way!

> BUBI *disappears.*

SCENE THREE

The clock starts to spin, lands on 3:59 p.m. From somewhere outside, the Chrismakkah CAROLLERS *start to sing. The singing wakes* ELY *up.*

ELY: Yo, Sarah, these pregnancy dreams are wild. Bubi was there and she was— Sarah? Sarah? Oh yeah. You're gone. Good.

> *The Chrismakkah* CAROLLERS *get louder and louder, and we see their shadows appear at the door.*

You've got to be bloody kidding me.

> ELY *heaves herself out of bed.*

I thought I told you unhinged cheerful bastards not to come back here!

> *She opens the door but there's nobody there.*

Hello? Chrismakkah Carollers? Hello?

> *She slams the door shut. Locks it. She hears her name being called, 'Elysheva, Elysheva'.*

Who is saying that?

> *There is the sound of hooves clomping. She turns back to the door, sees a figure with a reindeer headband.*

Carol? Carol is that you?

She shuts her eyes.

I never thought I would say this but ... please be Carol ... please be Carol ... please be Carol.

She opens the door. ADA *is there, and waves at* ELY. ELY *slams the door shut.*

What the what?

All the appliances turn on, shake, and make a lot of noise.

ELY *opens the oven.*

Bubi? You in there?

The oven bell dings once.

The oven bell!

The fridge starts to rumble, the fridge door bursts open, and out pops REIN-DYBBUK, *who has a cigarette in between their lips.*

REIN-DYBBYK: Got a light?

ELY: Got a what?

REIN-DYBBYK: A light, honey.

ELY: Are you a spirit?

REIN-DYBBYK: First things first.

REIN-DYBBUK *walks to the stove.*

This thing work?

ELY *nods.*

Give us a hand, love. I only have hooves.

ELY *takes the cigarette from* REIN-DYBBUK*'s mouth, lights it on the stove, and then returns it to the* REIN-DYBBUK*'s mouth.*

Much better! Now. You are— [*Consulting a rolodex*] Elysheva Scroogavitz. And I am the Rein-dybbuk of Chrismakkah past, yada-yada-yada you're my twentieth visitation today so come on toots, let's get this show on the road.

ELY: Yada-yada-yada? No yada-yada-yada.

REIN-DYBBYK: No good?

ELY: No good.

REIN-DYBBYK: Ugh. You want the spiel.

ELY: A spiel would be useful, yeah.

REIN-DYBBYK: They all want the spiel. Okay! I am a dybbuk, who has possessed the body of a reindeer. And no, before you ask, not Rudolph. That guy's a real / c—

ELY: Aren't dybbuks ... bad?

REIN-DYBBYK: Oh, yeah. Real bad. Anyhoo I have arrived to take you back to the past.

ELY: The past?

REIN-DYBBYK: Back to the past so you can figure out all your problems. In other words ... you.

ELY: You see, this is where everyone gets it wrong. They think I'm the problem. They think I can't stand on my own two feet. But that's exactly what I'm doing. Mastering the recipe, providing for my future.

REIN-DYBBYK: Totally.

ELY: Totally?

REIN-DYBBYK: Oh yeah.

ELY: So that's it? We good here? I can get back to work now?

REIN-DYBBYK: Yeah, sure, why not.

ELY: Really?

REIN-DYBBYK: No, you moron.

> REIN-DYBBUK *starts to make a noise: a smoker's cough intermingled with neighing.*

ELY: What is happening now?

SCENE FOUR

Christmas and Chanukah Eve, seven years ago. The bakery has transformed into a bustling, busy place. The shelves are suddenly stocked full of delicious looking pastries and breads and most importantly, gingerbread people. A constant stream of customers come to the counter. SARAH *is serving them, wearing a Santa hat.*

BUBI *and* FRAN *are at the bench.* BUBI *is making gingerbread.*

ELY *and* REIN-DYBBUK *watch on.*

FRAN: Mum, Dr Gluck is very concerned.

BUBI: [*Yiddish*] Az got hot geteylt dem seykhl bistu geshlofn. (When God was doling out brains, you were asleep.)

FRAN: You know I can't speak Yiddish.

BUBI: Pity.

ELY: Bubi! Hey ghost of Bubi, you're back!

REIN-DYBBYK: She's not a ghost.

ELY: She's not.

REIN-DYBBYK: That's what I said.

ELY: This is why I need the spiel.

REIN-DYBBYK: Fine. Christmas Eve. Seven years ago. Yada-yada-yada.

ELY: Christmas Eve seven years ago… What happened in the yada-yada-yada?

FRAN: Dr. Gluck …

BUBI: Dr. Shmuck …

FRAN: Says if you continue working like this you'll send yourself into an early grave.

BUBI: I'm ninety-nine. How early is early?

FRAN: Close the shop. It's the first night of Chanukah.

BUBI: I thought it was Christmas.

FRAN: It's both.

BUBI: It's a miracle! More holidays. More customers.

FRAN: I don't care about the customers.

BUBI: Good. Where are your keys?

FRAN: My keys?

BUBI: You don't care about the bakery so I guess you don't want the house.

FRAN: Mum!

BUBI: Or the car.

FRAN: Mum!

BUBI: Or the education, which, let's face it, didn't really work out for you.

FRAN: You're demented.

ELY: Hang on. I remember which Christmas this is. You are some messed-up dybbuk. No. I am not going back there. No way.

REIN-DYBBYK: Oh honey, I'd love to help.

REIN-DYBBUK *dresses* ELY *in a Santa hat.*

ELY: Do you hear me reindeer demon?!

REIN-DYBBYK: Rein-dybbuk. It's Rein-dybbuk. Oh, meant to ask, any heart conditions, motion sickness, epilepsy, pregnancy …

ELY: Um …

REIN-DYBBYK: Excellent. In you hop.

> REIN-DYBBUK *spins* ELY *into the scene.* ELY *starts baking alongside* BUBI. *They do this effortlessly, in synch. Meanwhile, the* REIN-DYBBUK *cruises around the space.*

ELY: Mum! Bubi! Enough with the fighting. [*To* SARAH] Hey, Sarah!

SARAH: Hey, Ely!

> ELY *turns on the radio. Christmas carols start to play.* ELY *and* SARAH *start dancing.*

FRAN: Aw. Aren't the girls sweet.

BUBI: If you think idiots are sweet.

> BUBI *turns off the radio.*

Back to work!

ELY / SARAH: Sorry Bubi.

> SARAH *returns to the counter.* ELY *returns to the bench.*

BUBI: And you can tell that Dr. Gluck to shove / his—

FRAN: Mum, I was lucky to get an appointment with him. Especially since your performance last time.

BUBI: He deserved it.

ELY: Deserved what?

BUBI: He had a little fall.

FRAN: She tripped him over.

BUBI: Who me?

ELY: Awesome.

> BUBI *and* ELY *high-five.*

FRAN: Just close already. I want us to be together.

BUBI: Are we not together?

FRAN: This is not together.

BUBI: And she thinks I'm demented? Here. Eat this.

> ELY *turns on the radio again.* ELY *and* SARAH *start dancing again.*

FRAN: Mum. You know I'm gluten intolerant.

BUBI: What did I do to deserve a gluten-intolerant daughter?

FRAN: What did I do to deserve a daughter-intolerant mother?

> BUBI *turns off the radio.*

BUBI: Back to work, Sarah!

SARAH: Um… I'm not actually getting paid for this.

FRAN: Mum! Pay Sarah!

BUBI: [*whispering to* ELY] But you know she'll come whether I pay her or not.

ELY: Bubbaliscious!

> BUBI *and* ELY *high-five.*

SARAH: Hey! I heard that!

FRAN: Ely, did you bake this batch?

> BUBI *and* ELY *look at each other and laugh.*

ELY: I wish.

BUBI: She wishes.

FRAN: Mum, get off your high horse already and give her the recipe.

BUBI: She's not ready.

ELY: I think I'm ready.

BUBI: [*mockingly*] I think I'm ready.

ELY: Come on, you old hag. Give it to me.

BUBI: No. It's like I always say, you want something / done properly you must do it yourself.

ELY / FRAN /SARAH: Done properly you must do it yourself.

ELY: Please, I promise I won't be shit.

FRAN: Of course you won't be shit.

BUBI: [*to* FRAN] You were.

FRAN: Mum! What if you want Ely to run the bakery one day?

BUBI: She'll figure it out!

> *The* REIN-DYBBUK *accidentally knocks something over and makes a loud bang.*

Now look what you've done, Fran!

FRAN: I didn't touch a thing! I wouldn't dare!

REIN-DYBBYK: Oops.

BUBI: [*Yiddish*] Ale tseyn zoln dir aroysfaln, nor eyner zol dir blaybn af tsonveytik. (May all your teeth fall out, except one to give you a toothache.)

REIN-DYBBYK: May all your teeth fall out, except one to give you a toothache. Savage.

FRAN: That's it. I'm leaving.

BUBI: No, I'm leaving!

FRAN: Finally!

BUBI: To pish!

FRAN: Argh!

> BUBI *storms off to the toilet. Fran storms out of the bakery. As she leaves she bumps into* BEN, *who is entering with some* CAROLLERS. *They start singing a Christmas carol. When they finish,* ELY *and* SARAH *clap.*

BEN: Thank you, thank you! We are the Jolly Christmas Carollers, here to spread joy with our smooth melodies and creative / harm—

BUBI: [*offstage*] Oi! Elysheva Scroogavitz, is that carollers I hear?

ELY: No! [*To* BEN] Sorry, what were you saying?

BEN: Oh … uh, yeah, so we are just popping and bopping around the neighbourhood / and—

BUBI: [*offstage*] Because if there are carollers there when I get off this toilet someone is going to pay for it …

BEN: Should we leave?

ELY: She'll be in there awhile.

BUBI: [*offstage*] And by someone, I mean Sarah.

SARAH: Why me?

ELY: She doesn't mean it.

BUBI: [*offstage*] I mean it!

SARAH: She means it.

BEN: Oh we should probably leave then …

SARAH: Yes.

ELY: No.

SARAH: Ely!

ELY: Customers, Sarah. Customers. You don't want to make Bubi more angry, do you?

> SARAH *shuffles back to the counter.*

BEN: Who's Bubi?

ELY: My grandmother.

BEN: I love grandmothers!

ELY: Not this one.

BUBI: [*offstage*] Fucking Christmas with its fucking songs about fucking tinsel and Santa and happiness.

BEN: Wow her voice really carries. [*To the* CAROLLERS] Hey guys. Do you want to go practice your Hallelujahs? You know the bit with the …

CAROLLERS: Okay, Ben. Sure, Ben.

The CAROLLERS *leave, practising as they go.*

BEN: I get it. Christmas is not for everyone. Personally, I just like the music but yeah. All the forced family stuff, the commercialisation of it all, the giant ham, the enormous tree, I mean for my mother the bigger the better. You know how it is.

ELY: We're Jewish.

BEN: Really?

ELY: Yeah …

BEN: Wow.

ELY: Wow?

BEN: So you don't …

ELY: No.

BEN: But your hat?

ELY: Have you met a Jew before?

BEN: No I have not! At least I don't think I have. But I could have. Of course I have because it's not like you guys all look the same and-oh-my-god-stop-talking-now do you have anything to add?

ELY: No. Keep going. This is fun.

BEN: Not to change topic but yes to change topic, isn't this place famous for its Christmas gingerbread. Or is it just gingerbread?

ELY: No, I believe it is Christmas gingerbread.

BEN: Gosh I'd love to try some.

BUBI: [*offstage*] Did he put in an order? If he didn't put in an order then he doesn't get my gingerbread.

BEN: Can I put in an order now?

SARAH *and* ELY *start laughing.*

ELY: [*loudly*] No you ignorant fool. How dare you ask for some gingerbread? What do you think this is? A charity for stupid people?

BUBI: [*offstage*] Good girl!

ELY: Psst! Sarah!

SARAH *throws* ELY *a gingerbread.* ELY *throws it to* BEN.

BEN: Is this ... are you ...

ELY: Are you scared?

BEN: Should I be?

SARAH: Yes.

ELY: Go on then.

BEN *bites into the gingerbread. His face is ecstatic.*

BEN: Oh. My—

ELY / SARAH: Shhhh!

BEN *finishes chewing while soundlessly miming his enjoyment of the gingerbread.*

BEN: Ahem. So. You're Jewish. That's ... that's ... cool.

ELY: It is?

BEN: Yeah! I mean ... not to sound ... Jesus. No not Jesus. Sorry. That was a weird thing to say. I love Jews! No that came out wrong. Your people are great! God, what is wrong with me? I'm just nervous all of a sudden. Am I sweating?

BUBI: [*offstage*] Elysheva Scroogavitz! Did you tell those singing imbeciles to fuck off yet?

BEN: She's great.

ELY: Um. Yeah. So. Anyway. Fuck off? I guess?

BEN: I'm Ben.

ELY: Ely.

BEN: Elysheva Scroogavitz. That's quite a mouthful. But I like it.

ELY: Why, what's your surname? Smith?

BEN: Um ... actually ...

ELY: Ben Smith.

BEN: Nice to meet you. So, Elysheva Scroogavitz, do you like Christmas carols?

ELY: 'Chestnuts Roasting On an Open Fire'.

BEN: Great.

ELY: 'White Christmas'.

BEN: Classic.

ELY: 'Santa Baby'.

BEN: Saucy. Love these.

ELY: All written by Jews!

BEN: Even better!

ELY: Oh, really …

BEN: Um haha yep so anyway, well maybe me and my merry band of carollers can arrange a special rendition … elsewhere … somewhere that's … not here … maybe … or not … or maybe the carollers don't need to come … I don't know just spit balling here …

> *The lights go out. Everything is in darkness, except for the* REIN-DYBBUK *and* ELY.

ELY: Wait! Where did you go? Where did he go? Ben! Ben!

REIN-DYBBYK: You're the one who said you didn't want to go back there.

ELY: I've changed my mind.

REIN-DYBBYK: Ugh. Humans. Fine.

SCENE FIVE

Ada's Bakery, six years ago.

BEN *is setting up Chrismakkah. He is fully decked-out in Chrismakkah clothes.* REIN-DYBBUK *begins to dress* ELY *in Chrismakkah clothes too.*

ELY: Ben!

REIN-DYBBYK: You know what would be good here?

ELY: A bedroom. Candlelight. A bit of Marvin Gaye.

REIN-DYBBYK: I was gonna say a saxophone solo but sure I'd be up for that.

> REIN-DYBBUK *spins* ELY *into the scene to join* BEN *in song.*

ELY / BEN: Happy Chrismakkah!

ELY: Ben and I have invented a new holiday … Chrismakkah!

BEN: A Christmas and Chanukah super festival!

SARAH: Yeah, sorry to burst whatever this is, but I think you'll find Chrismakkah was actually coined by the fictional character of Seth Cohen in the early oughts teen dramedy *The OC*.

ELY: Oy!

BEN: Humbug!

BEN / ELY: Oy humbug!

SARAH: Again another Seth Cohen reference, but sure.

BEN: Lots of singing …

ELY: Chrismakkah apparel …

> BUBI *enters.*

> ELY *throws everyone a Chrismakkah jumper, which* FRAN *and* SARAH *both put on.* BEN *tries to give one to* BUBI *but everyone shakes their head and he backs off.*

BEN: Dreidels …

ELY: And gingerbread people!

BUBI: Not my gingerbread people.

BEN: But Bubi, you make the best gingerbread people.

BUBI: For paying customers. Is he paying?

BEN: Um … yes? Cash or card, Bubi?

BUBI: Why is he calling me Bubi? Elysheva, what's wrong with him?

ELY: What do you mean?

BUBI: Why does he look like that?

ELY: Like what?

BUBI: So … happy. It's disturbing.

ELY: This is Ben, Bubi. I may have mentioned his name once or twice.

SARAH: More like one thousand or two thousand times.

BUBI: Not to me.

ELY: [*to* BEN] Early-onset dementia.

BUBI: What was that?

ELY: [*to* BEN] And hearing loss.

BEN: [*loudly*] My name is Ben.

BUBI: [*to* ELY] Are you sure there's nothing wrong with him?

BEN: [*loudly*] Nice to officially meet you, Bubi.

BUBI: If you say so. [*To* ELY] And what about his family?

BEN: Oh, it's just me and my mum, actually.

BUBI: [*to* BEN] Was I asking you?

BEN: No, ma'am.

BUBI: Where are they from?

BEN: From? From … here?

BUBI: [*to* BEN] Was I asking you?

ELY: His family are fine, Bubi.

BUBI: Fine until they murder you in your sleep.

FRAN: Don't mind her, Ben. And does your mother have plans for Christma— what were you two calling it?

ELY / BEN: Chrismakkah.

BUBI: Didn't I tell you all to leave?

FRAN: Well you must bring her here!

BEN: Oh … that's okay … she …

FRAN: Ben Smith. I won't hear of it. If she's anywhere as charming as you …

BEN: She isn't.

BUBI: Sounds like someone I know.

FRAN: Mum, please.

ELY: Fancy a song?

FRAN / SARAH: Yes!

> *Everyone starts to sing another Chrismakkah number.* ADA *appears and joins in. No-one sees* ADA *except for* BUBI, *who seeing her, grows very fearful. Midway through the song* BUBI *explodes.*

Enough! Enough! Get away!

> *The singing stops.*

This Chrisma— whatever this is. It's the most ridiculous, stupid thing I have ever seen. It's the type of simple-minded antics I would expect from Fran, but not you, Elysheva. Not you. What a waste of time. A waste.

ELY: Oy humbug?

BUBI: You have disappointed me, Elysheva. You too Sarah.

SARAH: Hey! Innocent bystander over here!

FRAN: That's it, Mum. Just ruin everything. Ruin every bit of fun this family ever tries to have. I'm leaving. I'm sorry, Ely, Ben. I just can't.

> FRAN *storms out.*

SARAH: No sorry to me?

ELY: Bubi …

BEN: Maybe we should … go?

SARAH: Sounds good.

ELY: We were just trying to have a bit of fun, Bubi.

BUBI: Fun? She thinks this is fun.

ELY: Yeah, fun, mucking around, like we usually do. Hey, Bubsy? Hubba Bubba? Bubbalicious?

ELY / SARAH: Scrub-a-bub-bub three bubs / in the—
BUBI: Shut up shut up shut up! Just shut up and get out of my bakery!

> *Everything is in darkness, except for the* REIN-DYBBUK *and* ELY.

> REIN-DYBBUK *is slow-clapping.*

REIN-DYBBYK: Bravo, bravo. You really pissed her off that time.
ELY: Are you … clapping?
REIN-DYBBYK: Trying to.
ELY: Our first Chrismakkah. We did that every year until he … until he …
REIN-DYBBYK: This is where the yada-yada-yada comes in handy.

SCENE SIX

Lights come up on Ada's Bakery, the 1990s. BUBI *is standing at the counter window.* REIN-DYBBUK *starts rummaging around looking for a drink.*

BUBI: [*to a customer*] Listen you putz. If you wanted three babkas then you needed to order three babkas, but my order sheet says two babkas, so you know what I'm going to do?

> FRAN *enters. She is heavily pregnant.*

I'm going to feed them to my dog, who will then die a slow, horrible death from chocolate poisoning you dog-murdering shlemiel, schmuck, az men shloft mit hint, shteyt men oyf mit fley. (If you sleep with dogs, you get up with fleas.)

FRAN: She doesn't have a dog! Honestly, Mum. What is wrong with you?
ELY: Seriously, Rein-demon?
REIN-DYBBYK: Dybukk.
ELY: I don't want to watch this.
REIN-DYBBYK: This is your past.
ELY: So where am I?
REIN-DYBBYK: Where do you think?
FRAN: [*collapsing into a chair*] This baby is going to be the death of me!

> BUBI *opens her mouth.*

Please, Mother. Do not say anything about how you hope this baby will be the death of me. Even for you, it's a bridge too far.

BUBI: Who me? I said nothing.

FRAN: The appointment is in an hour. Which gives you plenty of time to yell at approximately three more customers before we go.

BUBI: Who's we?

FRAN: We, is you and me.

BUBI: I don't have an appointment.

FRAN: It's not your appointment. It's my appointment. At the birth centre. Me. Your daughter. Your very pregnant daughter.

BUBI: What about what's-his-name?

FRAN: I can't get hold of him.

BUBI: Oy, you married such a loser. Where is he? At the dog track?

FRAN: He only ever went to the dog track because Dad took him there.

BUBI: I've told you not to speak of your father. What good ever came of that marriage I'll never know.

FRAN: I came from that marriage.

BUBI: Exactly.

FRAN: Are you coming with me to my appointment or not?

BUBI: Not.

ELY: Hey, can we wrap this up?

REIN-DYBBYK: This is the best bit!

FRAN: I've never asked for much but now— I'm not sure I can do this alone. I need you, Mum.

BUBI: I'm sorry, Fran. I've needed a lot of things in my life too. Did I get them? No. What can I do?

FRAN: This child is our future …

BUBI: Hmph.

FRAN: … Could bring us closer …

BUBI: Closer? How close is closer? You're breathing down my neck.

FRAN: Just share with me something, anything about your life, where you were born in Poland, who your family were, who Ada was—

BUBI: You are my family! I do everything for you! Do you not see? I've poured it all into this place. My blood. My sweat. My tears.

FRAN: Tears? None that I've ever seen.

ELY: And there it is.

BUBI: Aw. Poor Franny. Poor Franeleh. Franny wants me to cry.

FRAN: It's human.

BUBI: I don't have time to cry.

FRAN: Well, I guess you're not human then.

BUBI: Enough. My customers are waiting.

BUBI *takes some money from her purse and gives it to* FRAN.

Here. For the appointment. Take a taxi.

FRAN: Mum …

BUBI: Fran …

FRAN: Yes, Mum?

BUBI: A tropn libe brengt a mol a yam trern.

FRAN: What, Mum?

REIN-DYBBYK: A drop of love can bring an ocean of tears.

BUBI: You— You'll figure it out.

Everything is in darkness, except for the REIN-DYBBUK *and* ELY.

ELY: You'll figure it out?

REIN-DYBBYK: Families, eh.

ELY: I … I … I'm having this weird … like … feeling? I think I feel sorry for my mother.

REIN-DYBBYK: That is weird.

ELY: I don't like it, Rein …

REIN-DYBBYK: Rein-dybbuk!

ELY: What you said.

REIN-DYBBYK: Oh … okay … well … sorry-not-sorry about this next bit then …

SCENE SEVEN

Ada's Bakery, seven months ago. REIN-DYBBUK *spins* ELY *into the scene.*

ELY *is baking.*

SARAH *enters with a bag.*

SARAH: Hey, mate. How are you? I brought you some toothpaste, deodorant, fresh towels … Hang on. Are you baking?

ELY: Yeah.

SARAH: That's— That's great! Good for you. What do we have here? Cinnamon, honey, little people cookie cutters—hold up sugar-pie what are you baking?

ELY: Gingerbread.

SARAH: Gingerbread? As in Bubi's …

ELY: Yes. Gingerbread.

SARAH: Come on, Ely. If you're gonna get this place back up and running at least try something a bit more straightforward. Who knows what wizardry she used to make that stuff taste so good? God she was sneaky. What about a good old-fashioned chocolate babka?

ELY: Gingerbread.

SARAH: Apple strudel.

ELY: Gingerbread.

SARAH: Cherry danish.

ELY: Gingerbread.

SARAH: Cool, cool gingerbread it is. Okay, let me try some of Bubi's famous …

> SARAH *pinches some dough and tastes it. It isn't good.*

What in holy hell—

ELY: The recipe needs tweaking. She used to mix the cinnamon with the ginger and there was another spice she kept in a container under the bench which I can't seem to find and then the baking soda was a certain brand but I don't remember the quantity Sarah can you look under the bench or maybe it's in the fridge just help me Sarah, help me because I need to / figure this out …

SARAH: Hey, hey, hey. Ely. It's okay. I got you. Now where should / I—

ELY: I'm pregnant.

SARAH: Oh, there's the old Ely. Glad you haven't completely lost your sense of humour.

ELY: I'm not joking. I'm pregnant.

SARAH: What? How?

ELY: On my back, I'm guessing.

SARAH: Ew! With Ben?

ELY: No. Having a dead fiancé is apparently a real turn on.

SARAH: Oh, so …

ELY: Yes with Ben.

SARAH: Wow. Okay. So. Okay. That's. Yeah. Ely. Shit. Okay.

ELY: Sarah.

SARAH: Yeah?

ELY: Pass me the flour.

SARAH: The what now?

ELY: The flour.

SARAH: Come on.

ELY: And the eggs.

SARAH: Ely, we need to talk about this. Are you keeping it?

ELY: And the butter.

SARAH: I mean, what are you going to— How are you going to— Ely this is … this is huge. This is monumental.

ELY: And the sugar.

SARAH: Ely!

ELY: I'll figure it out.

SARAH: Figure what out?

ELY: I don't know! I'll figure it out!

SARAH *disappears. The bakery returns to its present state.*

REIN-DYBBUK *is trying to open the fridge door, but struggling with their hooves.*

REIN-DYBBYK: A little help!

ELY *opens the fridge.*

Cheers, darling.

REIN-DYBBUK *starts to step inside the fridge.*

ELY: What are you doing?

REIN-DYBBYK: Isn't it obvious? I gotta shoot.

ELY: Now? No! But I didn't figure it out! Please, stay!

REIN-DYBBYK: Look. I know you think we had a good connection. But honey, I'm a demon. Nothing good can come of this. Oh, which reminds me.

REIN-DYBBUK *hands* ELY *a form.*

ELY: What is this?

REIN-DYBBYK: A feedback form. Bureaucracy, right? Kills me.

ELY: …

REIN-DYBBYK: What's the problem? You can't read my hoof-writing can you?

REIN-DYBBUK *grabs the form off* ELY.

Hm. Neither can I. Basically, you went back to the past. You saw some shit. What did you learn?

ELY: I need to put better locks on the doors.

REIN-DYBBYK: Anything else?

ELY: That when my mum gets upset her voice does this / weird nasal—

REIN-DYBBYK: Did you learn anything … about life … the universe … et cetera?

ELY: Oh. Um … can't we just go back to the part with Ben? Like, it could be anywhere. The back seat of his car? The front seat of his car? We were quite good in cars.

REIN-DYBBYK: Meh. Lessons are overrated anyway.

REIN-DYBBUK *pushes* ELY *onto a large sack of flour.*

ELY: So we're going back? Do I look okay?

REIN-DYBBYK: No. And no.

ELY: But Rein-dybbuk!

REIN-DYBBUK *magics* ELY *to sleep.*

REIN-DYBBYK: That went well.

REIN-DYBBUK *magics* ELY *to sleep, and then steps into the fridge. The* REIN-DYBBUK *disappears.*

SCENE EIGHT

The clock starts to spin. The Chrismakkah CAROLLERS *start to sing. The singing wakes* ELY *up.* ELY *rushes as quickly as she can to the door.*

ELY: I thought I told you lot to piss—

No-one is there.

Okay okay you got me. You can come out now. No? Just gonna do the disappearing trick. Gotcha.

All the appliances turn on, shake, and make a lot of noise.

Oh oh oh here we go. Yep. Cool. Okay.

The oven bell dings two times.

And there go the bells. Love it.

As ELY *speaks, the giant gingerbread person sits up without* ELY *noticing, and is in fact, the Gingerbread* GOLEM*! The* GOLEM *has the Hebrew lettering emet (אמת) etched onto its forehead.*

So this is the bit that happens before whoever, or whatever you are comes to take me on a wild journey, or teach me some lesson, which so far, hasn't been all that useful! [*Looking around*] Okay. Out you come. Don't be shy. I'm not afraid of no ghost.

The GOLEM *creeps up behind* ELY *and taps her on the shoulder.* ELY *turns around.*

GOLEM: No need to be afraid, Mummy!

ELY: Ah!

GOLEM: Ta-da!

ELY: You— You're— You're my— You're alive?

GOLEM: Of course I am, Mummy.

ELY: Why are you calling me Mummy?

GOLEM: Because you made me.

ELY: No, I made a giant gingerbread person.

GOLEM: Yes.

ELY: Yes?

GOLEM: Yes. A giant gingerbread golem. That's right.

ELY: What?

GOLEM: I'm a golem. Your Gingerbread Golem of Chrismakkah Present. Hello. Do you love me? Oh please, please, please say you do!

ELY: Um … It takes me a while to warm up to people.

GOLEM: I take twenty minutes to warm up. Fifteen in a fan forced oven. And I am here for you. To help you … to protect you … to love you …

ELY: Oh, that's quite sweet / actually.

GOLEM: … To kill all the anti-Semites …

ELY: Wait, / what?

GOLEM: … and to taste good! What do you want? An arm? An ear? A foot. Both feet! It's okay! I can crawl if I need!

GOLEM holds out its arm. ELY takes a bite.

ELY: No no I don't think— Oh my god!

ELY takes another bite.

This dough is … How do you taste so good?!

GOLEM: Yummy, Mummy?

ELY: Now if I could just chop you up into little pieces and package you, I could save the bakery!

GOLEM: I mean you could … But probably better that we do the thing we're supposed to do first …

ELY: Which is?

GOLEM: Travel all the way to … now!

SCENE NINE

SARAH *and* RIVKA *enter the bakery.*

RIVKA: Hey Ely. Happy Chrisma— Do I have to say it?

ELY: For the last time, I'm not doing Chrismakkah!

GOLEM: You never told me that.

ELY: Not you! Them.

GOLEM: Oh them? No. They can't hear you.

ELY: Because…

GOLEM: You're not here.

ELY: So where am I?

GOLEM: In an Uber.

ELY: What?

GOLEM: Six centimetres dilated.

SARAH: She's not here? Typical. I can't believe Mum insisted we come back for Chrismakkah which, as I've been saying for years, Ely and Ben did not invent.

RIVKA: Are you really going to talk about *The OC* again?

ELY: Yeah, get a life, Sarah.

GOLEM: Yeah, Sarah.

SARAH: I mean, facts are facts.

RIVKA: Well, I can't believe your mum, going on and on about this Lilith thing. There's so much crap online. And the amulet. I think we need to be real. I mean, an amulet's not going to change the fact that Ely's an areshole.

SARAH / ELY: Rabbi Rivka!

GOLEM: Want me to get her, Mummy?

ELY: Maybe.

GOLEM: Just joking.

ELY: Same.

SARAH: No, I know. I do worry about how much time Mum spends on the internet.

RIVKA: This idea that Lilith is a demon who goes around stealing babies and impregnating herself with the spilled semen of teenage boys. It's all a bunch of archaic, misogynistic, antiquated concepts we've been forced to swallow.

SARAH: Please don't say semen and swallow.

ELY: So what? They're like … friends?

GOLEM: Best friends. Like us, Mummy.

SARAH: No, honestly, I love it when you talk dirty.

ELY: Hold up, what?

RIVKA: If I were gonna talk dirty I would not be saying anything about semen.

SARAH: I hear you.

ELY: OMG. Sarah and Rivka?

GOLEM: OMG.

ELY: Okay ladies get a room.

SARAH: There's a bed right over there you know?

ELY: Not my room!

RIVKA: Are you taking me into the closet?

SARAH *takes* RIVKA*'s hand and pulls her toward the closet.*

SARAH: Maybe …

ELY: How could I not have known?

GOLEM: Even I knew!

ELY: You knew?

GOLEM: I know things! I don't know how I know but I know things. For example, right now, your Uber driver is lost.

ELY: What?

RIVKA *pulls away.*

RIVKA: Hang on.

SARAH: What is it? I know it's gross in here but I can probably find an empty flour sack somewhere for / us to—

RIVKA: You still haven't told your mum about us.

ELY: She hasn't told Mum either?

SARAH: I— every time I try she just starts talking about Ely again.

RIVKA: Fucking Ely!

GOLEM: Are you sure you don't want me to get her, Mummy?

RIVKA: You are literally pulling me into the metaphorical closet with you!

SARAH: I mean, we don't have to go into the closet …

RIVKA: Sarah!

SARAH: I'm sorry! But Ely's gone full-blown bonkers. Did you see that giant gingerbread she was making? What the hell was that? And where the hell is that?

GOLEM: Over here, Aunty Sarah!

SARAH: Meanwhile I'm off having the time of my life, shtupping the rabbi.

RIVKA: I thought this was more than shtupping.

SARAH: It is! Of course it is! I love you! But if I tell my mother then she'll blab to Ely and hang on. Where is Ely?

ELY: I'm in labour. In an Uber.

GOLEM: And the driver is lost.

ELY: Yeah okay.

GOLEM: And you're now eight centimetres dilated.

ELY: Eight?

RIVKA: Ely's okay.

ELY: I am?

RIVKA: She's going to get through this.

ELY: I will?

RIVKA: She'll never recover from her grief …

ELY: Oh great.

RIVKA: But you can't stop living your life just because she's stopped living hers.

SARAH: It's just not that easy with my family and I think now isn't the right / time to—

RIVKA: There's never going to be a right time. Yes, your family is monumentally screwed up. And I've tried to help. Like, really tried. But I don't know how to be here as your lover and your support and your mother's support and now I'm getting hourly phone calls from Carol—I don't even remember giving her my number, and Sarah, you're forcing this relationship into a very dark place by not being honest about it.

SARAH: There's no room to be honest! There's no room for me!

RIVKA: You're wrong. There's no room for me. I can't do it any longer.

GOLEM: And end scene!

> *Lights go out on* SARAH *and* RIVKA.

ELY: No! They can't break up! No end scene!

GOLEM: Oh. Keep going?

ELY: Yes, keep going.

SCENE TEN

SARAH *is in the bakery alone.*

ELY: Where's Rivka? Oh no, Golem! Bring her back!

GOLEM: Hang on. Let me see …

> GOLEM *starts trying to magic* RIVKA *back.*

> FRAN *bursts through the door, bringing food and Chrismakkah decorations.*

Rivka!

ELY: Nope.

FRAN: Happy Chrismakkah, Elysheva!

SARAH: She's not here. I told you this was a terrible idea.

FRAN: Are you sure?

SARAH: Yes, I'm sure this was a terrible idea.

FRAN: And Rivka? I thought she was coming with you.

ELY: You did it, Golem! Rivka's coming back!

GOLEM: Yay!

SARAH: Rivka isn't coming.

GOLEM: Oh.

ELY: Good one, Golem.

FRAN: So what did I schlep all this Judaica for?

SARAH: Mum.

FRAN: What?

SARAH: Now that we're alone … You know, Rivka and I have become quite close.

FRAN: Rivka's lovely, isn't she? I'm very close to her too.

SARAH: Yes, I know you two are close. But her and I are … really close.

FRAN: It's not a competition, Sarah! Do you think we have enough latkes?

SARAH: I've been reflecting a lot on everything that's happened / this year…

FRAN: What am I going to eat? Does every Jewish food have to have gluten in it?

GOLEM: Guilty!

ELY: Sh!

SARAH: Mum, I'm trying to talk to you. It's important.

FRAN: It's important? Is it about Ely?

SARAH: Sure. It's about Ely.

FRAN: I'm all ears.

SARAH: After Ben died I couldn't make sense of what had happened. I mean, the day after they get engaged, he goes wildflower picking, alone, in the middle of nowhere, gets stung by a bee, and dies. Who does that?

FRAN: Ben.

SARAH: I found that talking to Rivka helped me. So I started going to synagogue more and spending time with her. And then … well … we … what I'm trying to say is …

FRAN: I know, Sarah.

SARAH: You know?

ELY: Oh, thank God.

FRAN: And to be honest, I'm moved that you want to share this with me.

SARAH: You are?

FRAN: It's deep.

SARAH: Yeah …

FRAN: Spiritual.

SARAH: I guess you could / call it—

FRAN: Sacred.

SARAH: I mean …

FRAN: The relationship between a rabbi and a congregant is very unique. It's the same for me.

SARAH: Oh, okay so. Nope. Definitely not the same. Okay. How do I say this so you get it? When Ely—

FRAN: Hang on. Where is Ely? Oh God. What if she's in labour? We need to call her! Call the hospital! Call the— Call the— Call Uber! Does Uber have a phone number? Sarah! Do something!

SARAH: What do you want me to do?

FRAN: Find Ely!

SARAH: No!

FRAN: No?

SARAH: No, Mum. I'm done. And you should be too. Here we are again, bending over backwards for her and she's not even here to appreciate it.

FRAN: Because she's probably lying in a ditch somewhere giving birth to my grandchild.

GOLEM: How does Mummy's mummy know you're in a ditch?

ELY: I'm in a ditch now? Whatever.

GOLEM: And fully dilated!

SARAH: Didn't you hear her yesterday? She's gone, Mum. She doesn't want to be around us. She said not to come back.

FRAN: Your grandmother said that to me a million times and I always came back.

SARAH: And where did that get you?

FRAN: What did I do to deserve this?

SARAH: Oh will you just shut up!

FRAN: Excuse me?

SARAH: Shut up shut up shut up!

FRAN: Sarah, what has come over you?

SARAH: Do you even see me?

FRAN: I'm not following.

SARAH: Did you even know that I deferred my studies to help look after Ely?

FRAN: Darling, you've been studying for the last ten years.

SARAH: Studying what, Mum?

FRAN: What?

SARAH: What have I been studying?

FRAN: The … well … first there was the … no hang on, that was Ely.

SARAH: Forget it.

FRAN: This is the worst Chrismakkah ever.

SARAH: Chrismakkah is over. Ely was right. Chrismakkah is dead.

GOLEM: And end scene!

Lights go out on FRAN *and* SARAH.

ELY: No! No end scene! Don't end the scene! Stop doing that! She didn't tell her anything!

GOLEM: Yeah, no. She didn't.

ELY: Why is it so hard for anyone in this family to say what they really mean?

GOLEM: Because of you, Mummy. Sarah can't tell Mummy's mummy about all the things in her heart because Mummy has taken up all the feeling space in Mummy's mummy's heart. So Mummy's mummy is sad and now Mummy's sister is sad.

> GOLEM *offers its hand to* ELY.

Bite?

SCENE ELEVEN

FRAN *is alone in the bakery.*

CAROL *appears outside, dragging a large Christmas tree.*

CAROL: Yoo hoo! Franny!

FRAN: What the hell is that?

CAROL: Franny! Open up!

ELY: Oh shit. Mum's going to kill Carol.

GOLEM: Kill Carol?

> FRAN *opens the door.* CAROL *enters and drags the tree inside.*

CAROL: Merry Christmas…kah Franny.

GOLEM: Kill Carol.

FRAN: It isn't merry anything.

CAROL: [*starting to sing*] 'Oh come, all ye faithful, joyful and triumphant, oh come ye, oh come / ye … '

FRAN: For goodness' sakes Carol, be quiet! I can't think with you banging on and I thought I told you not to bring a tree!

CAROL: Oh Franny. A bit of Jesus never hurt anyone. You people are so sensitive.

FRAN: You people?

GOLEM: We found one, Mummy!

ELY: One what!

GOLEM: An anti-Semite!

ELY: She's not an anti-Semite! She's the grandmother of my unborn child!

GOLEM: Oh! So, she's family.

ELY: Yes!

GOLEM: Got it, Mummy. I'll not kill Carol.

ELY: Thank / you.

GOLEM: Wink.

ELY: Wink? No, not wink.

> GOLEM *starts to stalk* CAROL. *Throughout the rest of the scene* GOLEM *comes very close to killing* CAROL *but misses every time.*

CAROL: Where's Ely?

FRAN: She's not here.

CAROL: She's not here? You don't think she's— The baby, Fran! The baby! The little wittle baby boo boo baby!

FRAN: The baby. I know! The baby!

CAROL: Oh, Franny! The baby! The baby!

FRAN: I know! The baby oh the baby!

CAROL: My precious little baby my darling my baby!

FRAN: 'My baby'? Pull yourself together, Carol! Who was I kidding? Chrismakkah is off.

CAROL: Off?

FRAN: Off.

CAROL: So we'll just do Christmas.

FRAN: Carol, I'm going to kill you.

GOLEM: I'm on the case, Mummy's Mummy!

ELY: No, Golem!

CAROL: Alright, what shall we do then?

FRAN: I'm not sticking around in this God-awful place, especially if I don't have to be here.

CAROL: Oh. Okay. I guess I'll just … grab my tree … it's not as heavy as it looks … don't worry I can manage … and take it the long way home … to my big … cavernous … two-storey … double-garage … empty, so empty, house.

FRAN: Alright then. Bye!

CAROL: Oh for God's sake Fran you're just as bad as the rest of them!

FRAN: Excuse me?

CAROL: You go on about how mean your mother was to you. Well, do you ever think about how mean you are to me?

FRAN: I don't often think about you, if I'm honest. I'm too busy thinking about my daughter, who is— God knows where she is.

CAROL: You don't realise how lucky you are, Fran. I buried my son, Fran. I held his cold cold hand. I shovelled the dirt onto his grave. And I carry that with me every single day. And soon, soon a grandchild will be born. I don't even know if I'll ever get to meet it.

FRAN: I don't know if I'll ever get to meet it.

CAROL: Don't be silly, Fran. It's your family. Your family. I've been telling myself that I could be a part of it. But if I'm really honest … and I know this might be hard for you to hear … I'm actually …

GOLEM: An / anti-Semite.

CAROL: Not sure how well I fit in.

FRAN: Family? I don't know what that is anymore. I thought if I held Ely close, if I loved her as I'd wanted to be loved … all this pain and sadness I feel would somehow go away. What a stupid woman I am. History repeats and repeats and repeats itself. You see? She's abandoned me just like my mother did. Now she's alone. And I'm alone. Sarah's alone.

CAROL: I'm so alone!

FRAN: So what's the point? What's the point in any of this?

CAROL: Come on, Franny. It's not too late. Let's find Ely.

FRAN: You know what, Carol?

CAROL: Yes Fran?

FRAN: She doesn't want me. She doesn't want any of us. I've spent my whole life doing things on my own. Now she can too.

CAROL: I don't want to be alone, Fran.

FRAN: In my experience, we don't often get what we want.

GOLEM: End scene!

   CAROL *and* FRAN *disappear.*

ELY: That's it?

GOLEM: That's it, Mummy. What's wrong?

ELY: They're all so miserable.

GOLEM: Me too. If only I'd been able to kill Carol. Cheer up Mummy. You got what you wanted, didn't you?

ELY: Which is?

GOLEM: To be left completely and utterly alone.

ELY: I guess you're right. But it doesn't feel how I thought it would feel.

GOLEM: Good. So you've learnt your lesson!

ELY: Yes, Golem. I suppose I have.

GOLEM: Good!

ELY: I'm delusional. They were right about the bakery.

GOLEM: Yes.

ELY: I'm the reason they're all so messed up.

GOLEM: Yes.

ELY: The only thing that will help is …

GOLEM: Teamwork! Yay Mummy! I will be rewarded for my good work!

ELY: … for me to disappear, completely.

GOLEM: Disappear? No, Mummy! I will be punished for my bad work! That isn't what we learned. No.

ELY: I've ruined everything. I need to leave.

GOLEM: Leave who? You don't mean me? You'd never leave me!

> GOLEM *clings on to* ELY.

ELY: Get off me!

> ELY *pushes the* GOLEM *off her and a piece of* GOLEM's *forehead falls away.*

GOLEM: Mummy, what have you done? You've ruined me!

> *The* GOLEM *disappears.*

SCENE TWELVE

The clock starts to spin. The Chrismakkah CAROLLERS *start to sing.*

ELY: Is that all you've got? I can't hear you!

> *The Chrismakkah* CAROLLERS *get louder and louder.*

All these ghosts and spirits visiting me but not the one I fucking want. Oh, what incompetent spirit is coming this time? A Shabbat elf? A prawn mocktail? Three wise yentas?

> *All the appliances turn on, shake, and make a lot of noise.*

Come on spirit! Let's finish this thing so I can be done with this place, once and for all!

> *The oven bell dings three times.*

And there it is.

A huge surge of wind blows the bakery door open. LILITH *is standing there.*

Okay … Hey. Hi. Hello. How are ya? Entering through the door, I see. How conventional. Long day? Yeah, tell me about it. So, you're a slightly different vibe to the other visitations I've had. I have to say the other two were a lot more chatty. But you. You kind of have this understated elegance. And I'm here for it. Why be all over the top with the woo-woo shit, right? Like we get it. You're supernatural. Why bang on about it? Um … Hello? … Cool, cool. So, I'm like, ready when you are. Fully ready. Let's do this thing.

LILITH: Lilith.

ELY: Hm? Say what now?

LILITH: I am Lilith.

ELY: You're Lilith?

LILITH: I am Lilith.

ELY: You see? My mum, she just exaggerates this shit. She was like, ooh, Lilith, she's so scary, she's gonna take your baby, she's gonna do wild stuff with semen or … no? Yeah, I didn't think that was a thing. Is it a thing? Should I not have sold that amulet on Gumtree? You can just chime in whenever you're ready.

The wind stirs.

LILITH: I have arrived to show you your future.

ELY: Great.

LILITH: It isn't great.

ELY: I didn't think it would be.

LILITH: Well, do you want to hear about it or not?

ELY: Babe, the quicker this happens, the better.

The wind builds.

LILITH: Elysheva Scroogavitz, you are destined for a cold, lonely, miserable life. A life without love. A life without warmth. A life without family. In the future, everything as you now know it will be gone. This place, your family heirloom. Destroyed. By you. Then, complete and utter destitution. You will suffer. You will hunger. A deep deep hunger that can never be satiated. Oh, you beg, oh, you borrow, oh, you steal. Your family doesn't come to your aid. No-one comes to your aid. Your own child abandons you. You end up with nothing. And then …

ELY: And then?

LILITH: The most, prolonged, humiliating, excruciating death.

ELY: Sure.

LILITH: In a biscuit factory.

ELY: Okay.

LILITH: With an industrial-sized cookie-cutter.

ELY: Fine.

LILITH: 'Fine'? No-one has ever said 'fine' before. Usually it's, 'no no no, Lilith'! 'Help me, Lilith'! 'I'll do anything you say, Lilith'! 'You're so beautiful and glamourous, Lilith'!

> BUBI *appears.*

ELY: Don't you see? My life is already over. How much more over can it get? So, come on demon lady! Just take me to my doom! I don't care! I just want to disappear! I just want this all to end!

LILITH: Delicious.

> LILITH *laughs and begins to sing a song pronouncing* ELY*'s impending demise, growing larger and more powerful.*

BUBI: No, Elysheva! You don't want this!

ELY: Bubi?

BUBI: I thought I told you to get your shit sorted.

ELY: This is me getting my shit sorted. I figured it out.

BUBI: Figured it out?

ELY: I'm no good to anyone. So Lilith is here. And she's going to finish it.

BUBI: Not Lilith. You need to finish it.

ELY: What's the difference? I need to disappear.

BUBI: There's no such thing as disappearing. Believe me, I've tried. You think you can leave your shit everywhere and it won't stink? It stinks! I left the bakery to you because I thought you could handle it. I thought you were strong like me.

ELY: I'm not strong like you. I'm nothing like you.

BUBI: We are more alike than you know.

ELY: How would I know?

BUBI: What?

ELY: How would I know, Bubi? You want me to learn a lesson about life? So teach me. Cos these other ghosts or spirits or demons are doing a pretty shithouse job. Zero stars review!

BUBI: Me?

ELY: You.

BUBI: She's right.

ELY: I am?

BUBI: It's like I always said, you want something done properly you must do it yourself. I swore I'd never go back.

ELY: Never go back to where?

BUBI: But maybe it's the only way.

ELY: Never go back to where, Bubi?

BUBI: Poland.

> BUBI *and* ELY *leave.*

> LILITH *swallows the bakery. She looks around, triumphant.*

LILITH: Huh? Where'd she go?

SCENE THIRTEEN

Poland, Christmas and Chanukah, 1938. Snowing, the forest.

ADA *runs into the forest and hides behind a tree trunk.* MISHA *rushes after her.*

BUBI: Ada!

MISHA: [*Polish*] Ada! Ada! Ada, where are you? You know I hate this game, Ada!

ELY: Ada? Hang on, Ada. As in *Ada's Bakery* Ada?

MISHA: [*Polish*] Fine. I'm leaving!

> ADA *pounces on* MISHA.

MISHA: [*Polish*] Don't do that!

ADA: [*Polish*] You're such a scaredy-cat.

MISHA: [*Polish*] And you're a … a … a …

ADA: [*Polish*] Watch out! She's getting angry!

ELY: A little help, Bubi? I can't speak Polish.

BUBI: Oy. Here.

> BUBI *magically makes them speak English.*

ADA: What did you think was going to happen? I was going to disappear into the forest, never to be seen again?

MISHA: Don't say such things!

ADA: Get struck by lightning.

MISHA: Stop.

ADA: Slip and fall into the raging river.

MISHA: Don't.

ADA: Get shot by a hunter. A policeman. A soldier.

MISHA: Your mother, more likely.

ADA: She doesn't scare me.

MISHA: She does me!

ADA: We are warriors, Misha!

MISHA: Like the Maccabees!

ADA: We will not listen to the ravings of a lunatic king!

MISHA: Turn off your radios!

ADA: Lock your doors!

MISHA: Arm your men, your women, your children!

ADA: Fuck you, Hitler!

MISHA: Sh! Quiet down.

ADA: Why? There's no-one here.

MISHA: There could be someone hiding behind a tree.

ADA: Who? A hunter? A policeman? A soldier?

MISHA: A ghost.

ADA: There's no such thing as ghosts.

ELY: That's what I thought.

BUBI: Sh! Just let me …

ELY: What?

BUBI: Remember.

ADA *hands* MISHA *an envelope.*

ADA: Happy Chanukah, Misha.

MISHA: You said we weren't doing gifts!

ADA: And you believed me?

MISHA: I left your gift at home.

ELY: Did you?

BUBI: Nope. She said, no gifts!

MISHA *opens the envelope and takes out a scrap of paper.*

MISHA: Two cups of flour. What is this?

ADA: Keep reading.

MISHA: Half a cup of— Hang on. This isn't what I think it is?

ADA: It is.

MISHA: Your mother's Christmas Gingerbread recipe?

ADA: Uh-huh.

MISHA: Wow!

ELY: Wow! This is where your gingerbread recipe is from?

> MISHA *is reading it.* ELY *tries to get a look at it.*

A little help, Bubi? I can't read Polish.

MISHA: Oh! I see! That's how she—

ADA: Uh-huh.

ELY: Bubi. Please!

ADA: Memorise it.

MISHA: Okay.

ADA: Got it?

MISHA: Yes.

ADA: Good.

> ADA *rips up the recipe.*

ELY: No!!!! Why???

> ELY *drops to the floor, trying to piece together the scraps.*

Why didn't you ever give it to me?

BUBI: You don't understand. I made a promise. I promised Ada to never show anyone.

ELY: What about your promise to me? To love me? To love all of us?

BUBI: I did love you. More than you know.

ELY: [*looking at* MISHA] I know she's you. But I don't recognise you.

BUBI: No.

ELY: You were …

BUBI: Happy.

MISHA: Your mother will kill you if she ever finds out you gave it to me.

ADA: We won't tell her. We'll move to Warsaw.

MISHA: Warsaw!

ADA: Open a bakery.

MISHA: Yes!

ADA: Making the most delicious gingerbread in town.

MISHA: We'll be rich! Ada and Misha's.

ADA: Misha and Ada's.

MISHA: Thank you. I love it.

ADA: Happy Chanukah, Misha.

MISHA: Merry Christmas, Ada. Your present's at home.

ADA: Sure it is.

MISHA: No! Wait! Happy Chris…

ADA: Ma …

ADA / MISHA: Chrismakkah!

> MISHA *and* ADA *start singing a Chrismakkah song* …

ELY: Oh, this just gets better and better. You came up with Chrismakkah?

SCENE FOURTEEN

JAKOB, RENIA *and* HALINA *enter with a chanukiah. They gather around to light it.*

BUBI: Look! Oh! Jakob! Mama! Bubi!

ELY: Your family?

MISHA / RENIA / HALINA / JAKOB: [*singing in Hebrew*] Baruch atah Adonai Eloheinu Melech ha-olam, asher kid'shanu b-mitzvotav, v-tzivanu l'hadlik ner shel Chanukkah.

RENIA: [*Yiddish*] Happy Chanukah!

MISHA / ADA: Happy Chrissmakkah!

HALINA: [*Yiddish*] Happy what?

RENIA: Speak Polish, Mum, so Ada can understand.

HALINA: [*Yiddish*] Es art mikh vi di kats fun mitvokh. (I care like a cat cares if it's Wednesday.)

ELY: Your grandmother?

BUBI: How can you tell?

ELY: Did none of you ever consider antidepressants?

BUBI: Did you?

MISHA: It's Chrismakkah, Bubi!

ADA: The best parts of Christmas and Chanukah combined!

HALINA: [*Yiddish*] What is she talking about? Az men tut on sheyn a bezem, iz er oykh sheyn. (Dress up a broom and it will look nice too.)

RENIA: [*Yiddish*] Mum, be nice!

HALINA: [*Yiddish*] What's the point?

RENIA: [*Yiddish*] The girl is harmless.

HALINA: [*Yiddish*] Suit yourself, but I'll be sleeping with one eye open.

ADA: I thought you all might like to try some of my mother's Christmas gingerbread!

HALINA: [*Yiddish*] She should go first.

RENIA / MISHA / JAKOB: Bubi!

HALINA: [*Yiddish*] What? You can never be too sure with these people.

RENIA: We'd love some, Ada.

ADA *shares the gingerbread around.*

HALINA: [*Yiddish*] Not bad. But have you tried my jam ponchkes?

RENIA: It's not a competition, Mum. Mm … Delicious! I must get that recipe from you, Ada.

ELY: Good luck with that.

BUBI: Sh!

ADA: Don't worry. The recipe is in safe hands.

ELY: Too safe.

MISHA: Ponchkes!

ADA: Gingerbread!

MISHA: What could be better?

JAKOB: Chrismakkah party!

JAKOB *turns the radio on.*

HALINA: [*Yiddish*] We'll wake the neighbours.

RENIA: Oh, Mum. Live a little!

They all dance. BUBI *and* ELY *join in.*

SCENE FIFTEEN

The family and ADA *crowd around* MISHA.

RENIA *is holding out a rucksack.*

RENIA: [*Yiddish*] There is some bread and cheese on the top.

MISHA: [*Yiddish*] Yes, Mama.

HALINA: [*Yiddish*] Eat the cheese first, or it will stink.

MISHA: [*Yiddish*] Yes, Bubi.

RENIA: [*Yiddish*] And you don't want to be known as the stinky girl.

MISHA: [*Yiddish*] Yes, Mama.

MISHA *starts to cry.*

RENIA: [*Yiddish*] Uh uh uh! No tears.

HALINA: [*Yiddish*] She mustn't cry. You cannot let them see you cry.

RENIA: [*Yiddish*] We are the strong women, right Mama?

HALINA: [*Yiddish*] Strong.

RENIA: [*Yiddish*] We have endured. And we will keep enduring.

HALINA: [*Yiddish*] Di velt iz sheyn nor di mentshn makhn zi mies. (The world is beautiful but people make it ugly.)

MISHA: [*Yiddish*] But why … why must I go alone?

RENIA: [*Yiddish*] Remember the plan. You go, study, and if things get worse, you keep going, and going, and going, and if you reach the end of the earth that's okay. You just keep going. And then you send for us.

HALINA: [*Yiddish*] You'll figure it out.

MISHA: [*Yiddish*] But Jakob?

RENIA: [*Yiddish*] I need Jakob here, with us.

HALINA: [*Yiddish*] Your Bubi isn't so young anymore, and as usual your deadbeat father is nowhere around. I hope you have better taste in men, my Misha.

> RENIA *puts the rucksack on* MISHA*'s shoulders.*

[*Yiddish*] Are the straps tight enough?

> RENIA *tightens the straps.*

RENIA: [*Yiddish*] Tight.

MISHA: [*Yiddish*] So tight.

RENIA: [*Yiddish*] Give your brother a kiss.

> MISHA *kisses* JAKOB.

[*Yiddish*] Kiss your grandmother.

> MISHA *kisses* HALINA.

[*Yiddish*] Kiss your mother.

> MISHA *kisses* RENIA.

Ada?

ADA: You have the recipe?

MISHA: [*Taps head*] In here.

ADA: I'll see you soon.

MISHA: So soon.

ADA: Goodbye, Misha.

MISHA: Goodbye, Ada.

>   MISHA *and* ADA *hug.*

[*Yiddish*] But what if I don't figure it out?

HALINA: [*Yiddish*] Enough of that now, or you'll miss your train.

>   MISHA *walks away, and then takes one last look at her family.*

SCENE SIXTEEN

Everyone disappears, except for ELY *and* BUBI.

ELY: Bubi?

BUBI: …

ELY: Bubi?

BUBI: I didn't figure it out, did I?

ELY: What happened? What happened to all of them?

BUBI: After the war I tried to find them. I posted notices in the paper. I wrote letters. To who? Who knows? The addresses I had were nothing but rubble. Silence. And then one day, I was in a café, having coffee, minding my own business, and in walks a woman I went to school with in Poland. And just like me, she washed up on this shore, right here, in this very town. Imagine that?

ELY: Ada?

BUBI: If only. This woman. You know, she was annoying as a child in Poland and equally as annoying as an adult and we never became friends …

ELY: Can you get to the point?

BUBI: The point is … the point is … Unlike me, she stayed. She witnessed: the ghetto, the deportations, the camps. And as I sipped my coffee she told me what I suppose, deep down, I had always known. When there was talk of the Germans' arrival, Ada convinced her family to take in my own. Imagine that! They only had a small apartment. But she was a mensch. They all were. Even the mother, who I always thought hated me. They hid my family until one day, some pig ratted them out, for money, or spite, or fun. Ada's family were punished, removed from their home, forced to beg on the streets. My family were put in the ghetto. And this woman, she was there the day they came to take them all away. My brother, my mother, my Bubi. And suddenly,

Elysheva, I couldn't taste my coffee. I sipped and sipped but tasted nothing. It was just mud, dirt, drek.

ELY: And then? Did any of them make it? Jakob. Ada? Someone? Anyone?

BUBI: Only me, Elysheva. Only me. That day in the café, my world was already a mess of language and hemispheres and oceans I could not swim the length of but that day, my world shattered into a million crumbs. Grief is a beast, Elysheva. It will eat you up. It will take hold of you. Possess you. Destroy you. Don't be like me, Elysheva. Face your grief. You must, for you, for your child. You see, you have the strength of your family behind you. All your family. Don't do what I did. Don't push them all away.

The ghosts of RENIA, HALINA, MISHA, ADA, *and* JAKOB *appear.*

History repeats, and yet does not have to repeat itself. We need to see our ghosts. Speak their names. I know that now.

The ghosts disappear, all except for JAKOB.

SCENE SEVENTEEN

BEN: Ely?

ELY: Jakob?

BUBI: That's not Jakob. That's Ben. You're welcome.

BUBI *disappears.*

ELY: Ben?

BEN: Hey.

ELY: Hey.

BEN: So this is weird.

ELY: Trust me, not that weird. Is it actually you?

BEN: Yeah. I mean … I'm dead but—

ELY *punches him.*

Ow!

ELY: Sorry! I couldn't help myself!

BEN: I had it coming.

ELY: Did I hurt you?

BEN: Nah! I'm still macho and tough. Get into all sorts of brawls up there.

ELY: Ben.

BEN: Some of those ghosts are scary, Ely!

ELY: Ben!

They hug.

BEN: I know it's not polite to ask and I'll understand if you'll want to hit me again but … is there a baby in there?

ELY: No.

BEN: Oh. This is awkward.

ELY: Yes it's a baby.

BEN: Wow!

ELY: Yeah!

BEN: And I'm the …

ELY: You drop dead and I'm flat out dating.

BEN: Well you were pretty feisty. I mean the backseat of my car got a real workout if memory serves me well.

ELY: Can't wait to tell the kid about her moment of conception.

BEN: Her?

ELY: That's what they say.

BEN: The next in the line of Scroogavitz women.

ELY: Yeah …

BEN: Geez that sucks.

ELY: Thanks a lot.

BEN: No I— It sucks that I won't know her. Will you sing to her? Maybe one of our Chrismakkah carols? Judolf the red-nosed Maccabee?

ELY: We both know that you were the real singer in the relationship but sure. I'll try.

BEN: I was the singer. You were the baker.

ELY: I don't know about that.

BEN: Really? But you were so good at it.

ELY: I've been trying to make Bubi's gingerbreads.

BEN: You found the recipe?

ELY: No.

BEN: Oh.

ELY: Yeah. It hasn't really worked out for me.

BEN: Those goddamn delicious gingerbreads. Who needs 'em, anyway?

ELY: Not me?

BEN: They were never that good. I think everyone was so scared of her, they bought them out of fear.

ELY: I know you're just saying that to make me feel better.

BEN: You feel better?

ELY: Are you less dead?

BEN: No, damn it! I'm sorry. I am so sorry, Ely. I'm sorry I walked into the path of a bee. I'm sorry I won't know our kid. I'm sorry we didn't get to say goodbye. I'm sorry I left you with my mother. I'm sorry.

ELY: That is such a lame thing for a dead person to say.

BEN: Sorry. How can I make it up to you?

ELY: By not being dead?

BEN: Is there anything else I can do?

ELY: I don't think so. Oy humbug.

BEN: Oy humbug. Do you want to hit me again?

ELY: Can we just hug?

BEN: We can do that.

> *They hug.*

ELY: You're not dating in the afterlife … right?

BEN: Oh no. You are the love of my life. And my death it turns out. But you … go for it.

ELY: You're not gonna watch or anything?

BEN: Oh, God no. I'll go and haunt my mother or something.

ELY: I love you, Ben Smith.

BEN: I love you too, Elysheva Scroogavitz.

ELY: Ben?

BEN: Yeah?

ELY: I feel like you're going.

BEN: I am? Maybe I am.

ELY: I don't want to be alone.

BEN: You're not alone, Ely. You've never been alone.

> *The Chrismakkah* CAROLLERS *start singing a Chrismakkah carol.*

Right on time.

> *Characters from* ELY*'s life and Chrismakkah journey appear.*
>
> *By the time the song finishes everyone leaves, and* ELY *is alone.*

SCENE EIGHTEEN

ELY: Oh shit.

> ELY *takes out her phone and dials.*

Mum? It's me. Ely. Yes, your daughter, Ely. Are you busy right now? Because I think I, ahem, need you? Yes. Yes, you heard me correctly. Mum, Mum, Mum! Maybe call Carol. She invited you to a movie? *Passion of the Christ* are you fucking kidding me? Well, call her. And can you call Sarah? And actually Rivka too. And tell them all to meet me at the hospital. Because I'm in labour. I could order an Uber or … You're what? You're outside? But how did you— Okay. Thanks, Mum. I'm coming.

THE END

Melbourne Theatre Company

BOARD OF MANAGEMENT
Chair Jane Hansen AO
Deputy Chair
Patricia Faulkner AO
Tony Burgess
Martin Hosking
Tony Johnson
Larry Kamener
Katerina Kapobassis
Professor Duncan Maskell
Sally Noonan
Chris Oliver-Taylor
Leigh O'Neill
Tiriki Onus
Anne-Louise Sarks
Professor Marie Sierra
Tania Seary

FOUNDATION BOARD
Chair Tania Seary
Deputy Chair
Jennifer Darbyshire
Jane Grover
Sally Noonan
Rob Pratt
Hilary Scott
Rupert Sherwood
Tracey Sisson

EXECUTIVE MANAGEMENT
Artistic Director & Co-CEO
Anne-Louise Sarks
Executive Director & Co-CEO
Sally Noonan
Executive Producer
& Deputy CEO
Martina Murray
Acting Executive Assistant to
the Artistic Director & Co-CEO
Cliona Kennedy
Executive Administrator to the
Executive Director & Co-CEO
Emma Vincin

ARTISTIC
Resident Director
Tasnim Hossain
Head of New Work
Jennifer Medway
Head of New Work (leave cover)
Matt Edgerton
New Work Associate
Zoey Dawson
First Nations Dramaturg
Bryan Andy
Playwriting Fellow
Jean Tong

CASTING
Casting Director
Janine Snape
Casting Associate
Rhys Velasquez

PRODUCING
Senior Producer
Stephen Moore
Programs Producer
Karin Farrell
Company Manager
Julia Smith
Deputy Company Manager
Lachlan Steel

DEVELOPMENT
Director of Development
Rupert Sherwood
Annual Giving Manager
Chris Walters
Major Gifts Manager
Sophie Boardley
Philanthropy Coordinator
Emily Jenik
Philanthropy Coordinator
(leave cover)
Moira Millar
Business Development
Manager
José Ortiz
Partnerships Manager
Portia Atkins

Partnerships Manager (acting)
Isobel Lake
Partnerships Coordinator
(leave cover)
Sidney Millar
Olivia Brewer

EDUCATION & FAMILIES
Director of Families &
Education
Jeremy Rice
Learning Manager
Nick Tranter
Education Content Producer
Emily Doyle
Education Coordinator
Brodi Purtill

PEOPLE & CULTURE
Director of People & Culture
Sean Jameson
People & Culture Executive
Christine Verginis
COVID Coordinator
Glen Sinnott
Receptionist
David Zierk

FINANCE & IT
Director of Finance & IT
Rob Pratt
Finance Manager
Andrew Slee
Assistant Accountant
Nicole Chong
IT & Systems Manager
Michael Schuettke
IT Support Officer
Darren Snowdon
Payroll Officer
Julia Godinho
Payments Officer
Harper St Clair
Building Services Manager
Adrian Aderhold

MARKETING & COMMUNICATIONS
Director of Marketing &
Communications
David Geoffrey Hall
Marketing Manager
Rebecca Lawrence
Marketing Campaign Managers
Grace Gaylard
Ashlee Read
Digital Engagement Manager
Jane Sutherland
Digital Coordinator
Isabelle Wawrzon
Lead Graphic Designer/
Art Director
Kate Francis
Editorial Content Producer
Paige Farrell
Editorial Content Producer
(leave cover) Tilly Graovac
Publicity Consultant
Good Humans PR

PRODUCTION
Technical & Production
Director
Adam J Howe
Senior Production Manager
Michele Preshaw
Production Managers
James Lipari
Jess Maguire
Production Administrator
Alyson Brown
Technical Manager – Lighting
& Sound
Kerry Saxby
Senior Production Technician
Coordinator
Allan Hirons
Production Technician
Coordinator
Nick Wollan
Production Technician
Operators
Marcus Cook and Max Wilkie

Production Technicians
Max Bowyer
Scott McAllister
Sidney Millar
Technical Manager –
Staging & Design
Andrew Bellchambers
Production Design Coordinator
Jacob Battista

PROPERTIES
Properties Supervisor
Geoff McGregor
Props Maker
Colin Penn

SCENIC ART
Scenic Art Supervisor
Shane Dunn
Scenic Artists
Alison Crawford
Colin Harman

WORKSHOP
Workshop Supervisor
Andrew Weavers
Set Makers
Sarah Hall
Nick Gray
Philip De Mulder
Peter Rosa
Simon Juliff
Welder
Ken Best

COSTUME
Costume Manager
Kate Seeley
Costume Staff
Jocelyn Creed
Lyn Molloy
John Van Gastel
Costume Coordinators
Carletta Childs
Matilda Woodroofe
Sarah Carr
Millinery
Phillip Rhodes
Wigs & Dresser
Kym McConville
Costume Hire
Liz Symons
Costume Maintenance
Jodi Hope
Susan Baksheev
Art Finishing
Claire Mercer

STAGE MANAGEMENT
Head of Stage Management
Whitney McNamara
Stage Managers
Jess Keepence
Vivienne Poznanski
Meg Richardson
Brittany Stock

SOUTHBANK THEATRE
Theatre Manager
Mark D Wheeler
Events Manager
Mandy Jones
Production Services Manager
Frank Stoffels
Front of House Manager
Drew Thomson
Lighting Supervisor
Geoff Adams
Deputy Lighting Supervisor
Tom Roach
Sound Supervisor
Joy Weng
Deputy Sound Supervisor
Will Patterson
Fly Supervisor
Sean Waite
Deputy Fly Supervisor
Cailum O'Connor
Stage & Technical Staff
Jon Bargen
Ash Basham
Al Brili

Suzanne Brooks
Connor Brown
Emily Campbell
Steve Campbell
Will Campbell
Charlie Craft
Jeremy Fowlie
Tallulah Gordon
Kylie Hammond
Adam Hanley
Justin Heaton
Spencer Herd
Chris Hubbard
Ethan Hunter
Julia Knibbs
Marcus Macris
Alexandra Malta
Jason Markoutsas
Terry McKibbin
David Membery
Seb Miloradovic
Maxwell Murray Lee
Sharna Murphy
James Paul
George Richardson
Jake Rogers
Natalya Shield
Darcy Smith
Jim Stenson
Nathaniel Sy
Dylan Wainwright-Berrell
Tom Willis
House Supervisors
George Abbott
Tanya Batt
Matt Bertram
Sarah Branton
Kasey Gambling
House Attendants
Rhiannon Atkinson-Howatt
Stephanie Barham
Emily Busch
Briannah Borg
Zak Brown
Sam Diamond
Liz Drummond
Leila Gerges
Bear
Hugo Gutteridge
Michael Hart
Elise Jansen
Kathryn Joy
Natasha Milton
Ernesto Munoz
Ben Nichol
Brooke Painter
Brigid Quonoey
Taylor Reece
Adam Rogers
Solomon Rumble
Sophie Scott
Mieke Singh
Ayesha Tauseef
Olivia Walker
Alison Wheeldon
Rhian Wilson

TICKETING
Director of Ticketing
Operations
Brenna Sotiropoulos
Customer Service Sales
Manager
Jessie Phillips
VIP Ticketing Officer
Michael Bingham
Education & Ticketing Officer
Melita Ilich
Subscriptions & Telemarketing
Team Leader
Peter Dowd
Box Office Supervisors
Bridget Mackey
Tain Stangret
Box Office Attendants
Tanya Batt
Sarah Branton
Olivia Brewer
Britt Ferry
Kasey Gambling
Min Kingham

Matisse Knight
Julia Landberg
Evan Lawson
Julie Leung
Nick Rose
Lee Threadgold
Rhian Wilson
Subscriptions Team Leader
Julie Leung
Subscriptions Officers
Daniel Alder
Stephanie Barham
Amy Dorner
Casey Gould
Hugo Gutteridge
Erin Hazel
Petria Hogarth
Min Kingham
Matisse Knight
Julia Landberg
Tom O'Sullivan
Isabelle Paci
Frederick Pryce
Cara Richards
Molly Webb

CRM & AUDIENCE INSIGHTS
Director of CRM & Audience
Insights
Jerry Hodgins
Database Specialist
Ben Gu
Data Analyst
Sionna Maple

ARTISTIC ASSOCIATES
Tony Briggs
Zoë Coombs Marr
Patricia Cornelius
Roshelle Fong
Kate Hood
Paul Jackson
Margot Morales
Stephen Nicolazzo
Zindzi Okenyo
Corey Saylor-Brunskill
Amy Sole
Sonya Suares

COMMISSIONS
The Joan & Peter Clemenger
Commissions
Kylie Coolwell
NEXT STAGE Commissions
Kamarra Bell-Wykes
Angus Cerini
Claire G Coleman
Patricia Cornelius
Roshelle Fong
Declan Furber Gillick
Dan Giovannoni
Sheridan Harbridge
Elise Esther Hearst
Matt Heffernen
Andrea James
Claudia Karvan
Phil Kavanagh
Benjamin Law
Kirsty Marillier
Nathan Maynard
Glenn Moorhouse
Kate Mulvany
Joe Penhall
Leah Purcell
Chris Ryan
Sally Sara
Melanie Tait
Aran Thangaratnam
Megan Washington
Mark Winter

OVERSEAS REPRESENTATIVE
New York
Kevin Emrick

Our Donors

We gratefully acknowledge the ongoing support of our leading Donors.

LIFETIME PATRONS

Acknowledging a lifetime of extraordinary support.

Rowland Ball OAM and
  The Late Monica Maughan
Pat Burke
Peter Clemenger AO and
  The Late Joan Clemenger AO

Greig Gailey and
  Dr Geraldine Lazarus
Allan Myers AC KC
  and Maria Myers AC
The Late Biddy Ponsford
The Late Dr Roger Riordan AM

Maureen Wheeler AO
  and Tony Wheeler AO
The Late Ursula Whiteside
Caroline Young and
  Derek Young AM

ENDOWMENT FUND DONORS

Supporting Melbourne Theatre Company's long term sustainability and creative future.

Leading Gifts

Jane Hansen AO and
  Paul Little AO
The Late Max Schultz and
  The Late Jill Schultz
The University of Melbourne

$50,000+

The Late Margaret Anne Brien
The Late Geoffrey Cohen AM
The Late Biddy Ponsford
Andrew Sisson AO and
  Tracey Sisson
The John and Myriam Wylie
  Foundation

$20,000+

Robert A. Dunster
Prof Margaret Gardner AO
  and Prof Glyn Davis AC

$10,000+

Jane Kunstler

PLAYWRIGHTS GIVING CIRCLE

Supporting the NEXT STAGE Writers' Program, our industry-leading commissioning initiative.

Paul and Wendy Bonnici & Family, Tony and Janine Burgess, Kathleen Canfell, Fitzpatrick Sykes Family Foundation, Jane Hansen AO and Paul Little AO, Larry Kamener and Petra Kamener, The Margaret Lawrence Bequest, Helen Nicolay, Tania Seary and Chris Lynch, Craig Semple, Dr Richard Simmie

The Vizard FOUNDATION

TRUSTS & FOUNDATIONS

Cybec Foundation

The Gailey Lazarus Foundation

HANSEN LITTLE FOUNDATION

The Ian Potter Foundation

NEWSBOYS FOUNDATION

telematics trust

trawalla foundation

JOHN & MYRIAM Wylie

VICTORIA State Government

Annual giving

Acknowledging Donors whose recent gifts help enrich and transform lives through the magic of theatre.

BENEFACTORS CIRCLE

$50,000+

Krystyna Campbell-Pretty AM
Peter Clemenger AO

Fitzpatrick Sykes Family
Foundation
Jane Hansen AO and Paul Little AO

Andrew Sisson AO and
Tracey Sisson O ●
Maureen Wheeler AO and
Tony Wheeler AO

$20,000+

Alan and Mary-Louise
Archibald Foundation ●

Edith Burgess
Tony and Janine Burgess
The Margaret Lawrence Bequest

Tania Seary and Chris Lynch
Craig Semple

$10,000+

Joanna Baevski ●
John and Lorraine Bates
Jay Bethell and Peter Smart
The Late Dr Jane Bird
Kathleen Canfell
The Cattermole Family
The Cordiner Family ●
Jennifer Darbyshire
and David Walker
John and Joan Grigg OAM
Linda Herd ●

Petra and Larry Kamener
Daryl Kendrick and
Leong Lai Peng (Betty)
Suzanne Kirkham
Macgeorge Bequest
Susanna Mason
Ian and Margaret McKellar
Helen Nicolay
Pimlico Foundation
Catherine Quealy
Janet Reid OAM and Allan Reid

Lisa Ring
Anne and Mark Robertson OAM ●
Dr Richard Simmie
Rob Stewart and Lisa Dowd ●
Three Springs Foundation
Ralph Ward-Ambler AM
and Barbara Ward-Ambler
Matt Williams – Artem Group
Anonymous (2)

$5,000+

Bagôt Gjergja Foundation
James Best and Doris Young
Paul and Wendy Bonnici
and Family
Bowness Family Foundation
Dr Douglas Brown and
Treena Brown
Dr Andrew Buchanan and
Peter Darcy
Ian and Jillian Buchanan
Bill Burdett AM and
Sandra Burdett
Lynne and Rob Burgess
Pat Burke and Jan Nolan
Diana Burleigh
Alison and John Cameron
Ann Cutts
The Dowd Foundation

Prof Glyn Davis AC
and Prof Margaret Gardner AC
Roger and Jan Goldsmith
Jan Green and
The Late Robert Green
Lesley Griffin
David and Lily Harris
Jane Hemstritch AO
Tony Hillery and
Warwick Eddington
Bruce and Mary Humphries
Sam and Jacky Hupert
Dr Sonay Hussein, in memory of
Prof David Penington AC
Jane Kunstler
Glenda and Greg Lewin AM
Helen Lynch AM and Helen Bauer
Martin and Melissa McIntosh

Paula McKinnon
Kim and Peter Monk
George and Rosa Morstyn
MRB Foundation
Tom and Ruth O'Dea ▥
Leigh O'Neill
Dr Kia Pajouhesh
(Smile Solutions)
Bruce Parncutt AO
Christopher Reed
Renzella Family
Lynne Sherwood
Tintagel Bay P/L
Marion Webster AM
Janet Whiting AM and Phil Lukies
Anonymous (6)

PROGRAM GIVING CIRCLES

○ **PRODUCTION PATRONS**   ▥ **YOUTH AMBASSADORS**   ● **EDUCATION**

ADVOCATES CIRCLE

$2,500+

Ros Boyce
Jenny and Stephen Charles AO
Geoff Cosgriff ●
Susanne Dahn
Ann Darby ○ ●
Megan Davis and Antony Isaacson
The Dodge Family Foundation
Rodney Dux
Melody and Jonathan Feder
Anna and John Field
Jan and Rob Flew
Nigel and Cathy Garrard
Diana and Murray Gerstman
Charles Gillies and Penny Allen
Heather and Bob Glindemann OAM
Henry Gold
Jane Grover

Halina Lewenberg Charitable
    Foundation
Peter and Halina Jacobsen
Josephine and Graham Kraehe AO
Leg Up Foundation ▦
Lording Family Foundation
Virginia Lovett and
    Rose Hiscock ○
Professor Duncan Maskell and
    Dr Sarah Maskell
Margaret and John Mason OAM
Don and Sue Matthews
John G Millard and Andrew Cason
Sandra Murdoch
Jane and Andrew Murray
Nelson Bros Funeral Services
The Orloff Family Charitable Trust
Roger and Ruth Parker

Jeremy Ruskin and Roz Zalewski
In memory of Marysia and
    Berek Segan AM OBE
Prof Barry Sheehan and
    Pamela Waller
Brian Snape AM and
    Christina Martin
Geoff Steinicke
Ricci Swart AM
James and Anne Syme
Richard and Debra Tegoni ●
Liz Tromans
The Veith Foundation
Price and Christine Williams
The Ray and Margaret Wilson
    Foundation
Gillian and Tony Wood
Anonymous (4)

LOYALTY CIRCLE

$1,000+

Prof Noel Alpins AM and
    Sylvia Alpins
Margaret Astbury
Ian Baker and Cheryl Saunders
John and Dagnija Balmford
Prof Robin Batterham
Sandra Beanham

Judy Bourke ●
Steve and Terry Bracks AM
Jenny and Lucinda Brash
Bernadette Broberg
Nigel and Sheena Broughton
Beth Brown and
    The Late Tom Bruce AM
Nan Brown
Rob and Sal Bruce
Julie Burke
Katie Burke
Geoffrey Bush and
    Michael Riordan
Pam Caldwell
Helen and Dugald Campbell
John and Jan Campbell
Jessica Canning
Clare Carlson
Fiona Caro
Chernov Family
Keith Chivers and Ron Peel
Assoc Prof Lyn Clearihan AM and
    Dr Anthony Palmer
Sandy and Yvonne Constantine
Jutta Cowen

Karen Cusack
Natasha Davies
Megan Davis and Antony Isaacson
Sue and John Denmead
Katharine Derham Moore
Dr Anthony Dortimer and
    Jillian Dortimer
Robert Drake
Mark Duckworth PSM and
    Lauren Moss
Dr Sally Duguid and
    Dr David Tingay
Pam Durrant
Bev and Geoff Edwards
Karen and David Elias
George and Eva Ermer
Anne Evans and Graham Evans AO
Marian Evans
Dr Alastair Fearn
Peter Fearnside and
    Roxane Hislop
Peter and Mary Fildes
Grant Fisher and Helen Bird ●
Rosemary Forbes and Ian Hocking
Bruce Freeman ▦
Dr Justin Friebel and Jessica Rose
John R Fullerton
Gaye and John Gaylard
Gill Family Foundation
Fiona Griffiths and Tony Osmond
Ian and Wendy Haines
Charles Harkin
M D Harper

Mark and Jennifer Hayes ●
Luke Heagerty
Lorraine Hendrata
Brett and Kerri Hereward
Dr Alice Hill and Mark Nicholson
Emeritus Prof Andrea Hull AO
Nanette Hunter
Ann and Tony Hyams AM
Will and Jennie Irving
Peter Jaffe and Judy Gold
Neil Jens ●
Ben Johnson and Mark McNamara
Ed and Margaret Johnson
Sally and Rod Johnstone
Leah Kaplan and Barry Levy
Irene Kearsey and Michael Ridley
Malcolm Kemp
Daniel Kilby
Fiona Kirwan-Hamilton and
    Brett Parkin
Doris and Steve Klein
Marianne and Arthur Klepfisz
Larry Kornhauser and
    Natalya Gill ● ▦
Anne Le Huray
Verona Lea
Joan Lefroy AM and
    George Lefroy AM
Alison Leslie
Peter and Judy Loney
Lord Family
Kerryn Lowe and Raphael Arndt
Elizabeth Lyons

PROGRAM GIVING CIRCLES

○ PRODUCTION PATRONS   ▦ YOUTH AMBASSADORS   ● EDUCATION

Ken and Jan Mackinnon
Karin MacNab
Chris and Bruce Maple
Ian and Judi Marshman
Penelope McEniry
Heather and Simon McKeon ■
Garry McLean
Libby McMeekin
Emeritus Prof Peter McPhee AM
Rosemary Meagher and
   The Late Douglas Meagher
Robert and Helena Mestrovic
Ann Miller AM
Ross and Judy Milne-Pott
MK Futures
Barbara and David Mushin
Sarah Nguyen
Nick Nichola and Ingrid Moyle
Dr Paul Nisselle AM and
   Sue Nisselle
Sally Noonan
David and Lisa Oertle
Dr Jane and Alan Oppenheim
Arthur Ozols
In loving memory of Richard Park

Dr Annamarie Perlesz
Peter Philpott and Robert Ratcliffe
Philip and Gayle Raftery
David Reckenberg and
   Dale Bradbury
Sally Redlich
Victoria Redwood
Veronica and John Rickard ●
Phillip Riggio
Ken and Gail Roche ●
Roslyn and Richard Rogers
   Family ●
S and S Rogerson
B and J Rollason
Sue Rose
Nick and Rowena Rudge
Jenny Russo
Edwina Sahhar
Margaret Sahhar AM
Alex & Brady Scanlon Giving Fund
Sally and Tim Scott
Jacky and Rupert Sherwood
Diane Silk
Dr John Sime
Pauline and Tony Simioni

Jan Simon
Jane Simon and Peter Cox
Tim and Angela Smith
Annette Smorgon
Dr Ross and Helen Stillwell
The Stobart Strauss Foundation
Irene and John Sutton
Christopher Swan ●
Rodney and Aviva Taft
Frank Tisher OAM and
   Dr Miriam Tisher
John and Anna van Weel
Graham Wademan and
   Michael Bowden
Walter and Gertie Wagner ●
Kevin and Elizabeth Walsh ■
Pinky Watson
Kaye and John de Wijn ●
Ann and Alan Wilkinson ●
Robert and Diana Wilson
Ralph Wollner and
   The Hon Kirsty Macmillan SC
Mandy and Edward Yencken
Anonymous (24)

LEGACY CIRCLE

Acknowledging supporters who have made the visionary gesture of including
a gift to Melbourne Theatre Company in their will.

John and Lorraine Bates
Mark and Tamara Boldiston
Bernadette Broberg
Adam and Donna Cusack-Muller
Anne Evans and Graham Evans AO
Bruce Freeman
Peter and Betty Game
Edith Gordon

Fiona Griffiths
Linda Herd
Tony Hillery and
   Warwick Eddington
Jane Kunstler
Irene Kearsey
Robyn and Maurice Lichter

Dr Andrew McAliece and
   Dr Richard Simmie
Libby McMeekin
Peter Philpott and Robert Ratcliffe
Marcus Pettinato
Jillian Smith
Diane Tweeddale
Anonymous (17)

PROGRAM GIVING CIRCLES

○ **PRODUCTION PATRONS**   ■ **YOUTH AMBASSADORS**   ● **EDUCATION**

Current as of October 2023. For more information about supporting Melbourne Theatre Company
please contact our Philanthropy team at **donations@mtc.com.au** or visit **mtc.com.au/support**

Thank you

Melbourne Theatre Company would like to thank the following organisations for their generous support.

Major Partner

Future Directors Initiative Partner

MinterEllison.

Major Marketing Partners

oOh! unmissable

The Monthly
The Saturday Paper
7am

Presenting Partner

THE LANGHAM
MELBOURNE

Associate Partners

Challis & Company
Tomorrow's leaders today

Frontier
software
Human Capital Management
& Payroll Software/Services

K&L GATES

LITTLE
GROUP

Supporting Partners

COMMITTEE
MELBOURNE FOR

Genovese
COFFEE

KAWAI

THE
LUXURY
NETWORK®

METROPOLIS
EVENTS

QUEST
SOUTHBANK

SOH
MELBOURNE

taxi kitchen

Wilson Parking

Marketing Partners

● BROADSHEET

CINEMA
NOVA

invicium

southgate

RRR

Southbank Theatre Partners

mgc
THE
MELBOURNE
GIN COMPANY

SCOTCHMANS HILL
BELLARINE PENINSULA
VICTORIA
ESTABLISHED 1982

Current as of October 2023. To learn more about partnership opportunities at Melbourne Theatre Company or to host a private event, please contact **partnerships@mtc.com.au**

www.currency.com.au

Visit Currency Press' website now to:

- Buy your books online
- Browse through our full list of titles, from plays to screenplays, books on theatre, film and music, and more
- Choose a play for your school or amateur performance group by cast size and gender
- Obtain information about performance rights
- Find out about theatre productions and other performing arts news across Australia
- For students, read our study guides
- For teachers, access syllabus and other relevant information
- Sign up for our email newsletter

The performing arts publisher

www.ingramcontent.com/pod-product-compliance
Lightning Source LLC
Chambersburg PA
CBHW050020090426
42734CB00021B/3346